To John + Joy.

with best wishes.

On Being Saved

The Roots of Redemption

Rod Garner

DARTON · LONGMAN + TODD

First published in 2011 by
Darton, Longman and Todd Ltd
1 Spencer Court
140 – 142 Wandsworth High Street
London SW18 4JJ

ISBN: 978-0-232-52836-7

A catalogue record for this book is available from the British Library

Phototypeset by Kerrypress Ltd, Luton, Bedfordshire

Printed and bound in Great Britain by Page Bros, Norwich, Norfolk.

For Sister Laura and her companions at Ince Blundell Hall. With gratitude and affection for their hospitality and their house of prayer.

·❦·

Contents

Introduction

For a number of good reasons this feels the right time to share some sustained thoughts on the religious meaning of redemption. A cold economic climate and harder times are increasingly concentrating minds on things that really matter. The wealth of a nation amounts to more than its bank deposits and there is a growing awareness that happiness and human well-being cannot be measured in financial terms alone. I also find it interesting and significant that unlike other key religious terms that have been carelessly or conveniently discarded from the language – sin, judgement and contrition come readily to mind here – the idea of salvation and the longing to be saved retain a hold on the heart and the imagination. If we seem less than clear concerning what might make us whole, we are in no doubt about the hurts and agitations that deny our ease or the sense that a truer and more satisfying life might still be eluding us.

For centuries the Christian gospel has spoken to such tensions, often with authority and success. Countless lives have been transformed or changed for the better by the healing power of scripture or the irresistible holiness of saintly lives. Others have felt the presence of the Holy Spirit and, in the words of John Wesley, have been led on 'to explore the unfathomable wonders of what it is to be an adopted child of God'. Many have come to the foot of the cross and have discovered, in the wounded head of Christ and his suffering, the fulfilment of their deepest needs. Such transformations continue and thriving congregations are nourished by traditional signs and symbols and the experience of being redeemed by the precious blood of their Saviour. Beyond the churches, however, there is a different story to be told. Questioning, sceptical or indifferent minds seem quite unmoved by our melodies and often disconcerted by the cruel sacrifice that seems to lie at the heart of much Christian teaching concerning redemption. Instinctively, they sense that there is more to be said about salvation and human wholeness than the shedding of blood, the fear of divine judgement or the lure of a hereafter. The argument of this book runs in their direction – that there is indeed a lot more to be said than the pulpit, or one-dimensional preaching, can normally muster.

In this respect I recognise two perennial concerns in my ministry as priest and teacher: a duty on the one hand to take seriously the world's questions and objections in matters of faith and, on the other, a passion to present the gospel in a way that speaks to the hopes and confusions of our time. I am persuaded with T. S. Eliot that 'Christianity must forever be adapting itself into that which can be believed' and in what follows my aim is to illuminate the common ground that links the mystery of our humanity to the greater mystery of God. There is also a personal agenda. With the passage of time and the inevitable weight of laments, tragedies and failures that must attend any authentic pastoral ministry that looks upon the world as its parish, the question of what we may hope for in this life when too often goodness and truth are overshadowed by wickedness and lies is never far from my mind. I remain hopeful and sometimes happy but I do realise that at one level this book is an attempt to banish the demons at my shoulder that are not disposed to give me peace!

In terms of what you will find in these pages, I begin by affirming the essential goodness of human life in contrast to the excessively negative view that has too often characterised Christianity. Attention is paid to our capacity for waywardness and our startling ability to get things wrong. To know 'on the pulse', so to speak, that we are by nature some way off perfection is in itself a liberating truth. Morally speaking, we are all work in progress and that fact alone can make us more forgiving of our own failures and those of others. Two chapters concentrate on suffering – how could it be otherwise when a 'man of sorrows' haunts our religious imagination, and torments of various kinds afflict too many lives? The significance of the cross is re-evaluated along with our own responses to suffering. Memory, beauty and laughter take up three chapters and they are celebrated as things of great redemptive worth. Beyond the saving acts of Christ, the reader is also challenged to see the work of redemption as something we engage in for the sake of the world. A final chapter explores hope and how, in the end, it proves more contagious than despair. Poets, philosophers, writers, musicians and artists all play a part between these covers along with the dependable and durable insights of scripture and theology. Taken together, they help and encourage me to view redemption from a broader and deeper perspective. I shall be more than satisfied if they assist you to do the same.

In the year or so that went into the writing of this book, sickness and hospitalisation on the part of those very close to me loomed large for several months. The 'pause' button had to be pressed several times on the project and it is a small miracle that the manuscript reached my editor, Virginia Hearn, fairly close to the deadline! Her understanding and encouragement have been much appreciated. I am particularly grateful to the Augustinian Sisters at Ince Blundell Hall, Merseyside. When I needed space to write and pray, I was blessed by their chapel, their hospitality and a room of my own. I thank God for them. Ruby Smith also kept faith with me in a difficult time and managed, yet again, to decipher handwriting that would baffle the best and translate it into intelligible prose! She has my thanks and admiration.

Rod Garner
Advent 2010

CHAPTER 1

Liberating the Gospel

I'm reading Raymond Carver again. I keep his poems by the bedside, close to hand for when I need them. Carver was born in Oregon, USA, in 1938. He married young and made a living as a hospital porter, dictionary salesman, petrol station attendant and delivery man. For years writing had come second to the demands of marriage and raising a family. He managed to enrol for a creative writing course but his small body of published work increasingly reflected the personal and domestic pressures that were threatening to over-whelm him. He turned to alcohol, which eventually contributed to the breakdown of his marriage. In 1977 he stopped drinking and also met another poet, Tess Gallagher, with whom he shared the last eleven years of his life. He began to write again – collections of short stories and poetry – and months before his death in 1988 he was inducted into the American Academy of Arts and Letters.

A New Path to the Waterfall[1] is my bedside companion and it includes his last poems, written following his diagnosis with lung cancer in September 1987. The months that followed were hard but fruitful. He was not ready to die at 50 and, as the cancer quickened, he wrote in a journal: 'I wish I had a while. Not five years – or even three years – I couldn't ask for that long, but if I had even a year. If I knew I had a year'[2]. There was no intervention or remission but, alongside the fears and griefs of parting, he found a happiness and peace that had often eluded his earlier years. He savoured times of recollection, celebrated his eleven years together with Tess by marrying her in a private ceremony in Reno, Nevada and wrote the poems in which he came 'to feel myself beloved on the earth'[3]. He made use of the best that was in him but, even as he hoped that more days would come, he wrote on the packs of his cigarettes the imperative 'NOW'.

At one level, Carver knew that he was a lucky man. Before meeting Tess his drinking had seemed certain to destroy him. But he recovered and found in her his bright morning star. *A New Path to the Waterfall* is dedicated to her. Four words suffice: 'Tess. Tess. Tess. Tess.' She enabled him to delight in the gift of the present and, finally, celebrate love in the face of death:

> I see an empty place at the table.
> Whose? Who else's? Who am I kidding?
> The boat's waiting. No need for oars
> or a wind. I've left the key
> in the same place. You know where.
> Remember me and all we did together.
> Now, hold me tight. That's it. Kiss me
> hard on the lips. There. Now
> let me go my dearest. Let me go.
> We shall not meet again in this life,
> so kiss me goodbye now. Here, kiss me again.
> Once more. There. That's enough.
> Now, my dearest, let me go.
> It's time to be on the way.[4]

Tess, unwittingly, enacted the instructions of this poem on the night before his death. She kissed him three times, encouraged him to sleep and said, finally, 'I love you'. Raymond uttered the same words and, at 6.20 the next morning, he died

Why am I drawn back again and again to this stumbling yet deeply gifted writer? There is, first of all, his humanity. His failings and contradictions at no point contaminate his truth-seeking heart. Poetry is for him a spiritual necessity and his words in their disarming simplicity and directness convey the ache and awe of living in this world. Readers from different countries mailed letters and cards to his home at his passing, expressing gratitude for things he had said or stories they had shared. It is hard not to feel affection and admiration for a man who, on learning that he is going to die, can write the following:

> He said it doesn't look good
> he said it looks bad in fact real bad
> he said I counted thirty-two of them on one lung before
> I quit counting them

I said I'm glad I wouldn't want to know
about any more being there than that
he said are you a religious man do you kneel down
in forest groves and let yourself ask for help
when you come to a waterfall
mist blowing against your face and arms
do you stop and ask for understanding at those moments
I said not yet but I intend to start today.[5]

Most of us would fall apart on receiving such news but Carver is able to recall the pathos of the encounter – the doctor conveying a fatal diagnosis and a patient suddenly discovering a renewed desire to pray in the knowledge of his mortality. The whole poem is deeply affecting and in its restraint and courtesy (Carver shakes the doctor's hand and thanks him before leaving) it somehow manages to soften a meeting that ostensibly offers only dread. Without sentimentality, artifice or evasion it embraces the unpalatable and unthinkable and denies them the last word. It holds on to the graced possibilities of the most feared human encounter and finds a strange richness in sorrow. Most of us are wasters of sorrow but Carver grasped that there can be no fulfilled or genuinely happy life without confronting at some point heartache or tragedy.

To read his poetry and stories is to discover that nothing is alien to him and everything is of interest. He notices things that little bit better than most of us as we move through life and sets them down with warmth and emotion. He can recall the sight of a woman bathing or the huge fish he saw as a child on a visit with his father to an exhibition. He is engrossed by the state of his toes and what it was once like to be 'first on to the dance floor when the music started'[6]. He contemplates with pleasure the shapely nylon stockings left by his wife on the bed and is intoxicated by the heavy smell of crocuses or the sight of rooks floating over fields. It is a generous vision informed by the spirit of life that is in him and the urgent desire to taste and see:

Make use of the things around you.
This light rain
Outside the window, for one.
This cigarette between my fingers.

These feet on the couch.
The faint sound of rock and roll,
The red Ferrari in my head.
The woman bumping
Drunkenly around the kitchen ...
Put it all in,
Make use.[7]

There is something redemptive at work here that for me, along with
his humanity, explains why I continue to return to Carver. Put
simply, he points us to the potency of ordinary moments – the falling
rain, the sound of distant music, the fire of the imagination (the red
Ferrari in my head) – that can illuminate the most remarkable
things. To this endeavour he brings his own unusual gifts, tempered
by his reading of other poets who have influenced him. *A New Path to
the Waterfall* opens with the poem 'Gift' by Czeslaw Milosz:

A day so happy.
Fog lifted early, I worked in the garden.
Humming birds were stopping over honeysuckle flowers.
There was nothing on earth I wanted to possess.
I knew no one worth my envying him.
Whatever evil I had suffered, I forgot.
To think that once I was the same man
did not embarrass me.
In my body I felt no pain.
When straightening up, I
saw the blue sea and sails.

I want to encourage you to pause at this point and to re-read the
above lines before continuing. They recall in a quite perfect way a
present moment where now is all that seems to matter and all
agitations melt away. In a world of much contrariness and pain they
affirm that it is still possible to feel ourselves 'beloved on the earth'.
Let me try and put this in more personal terms. In the late autumn of
2008, along with my wife Christine, I spent some time on the
campus of Berkeley University, California. When I was not working
it was a joy – no other word for it – to walk in the warm sunshine,
admire the stunning buildings and clock tower and be renewed by

the sights and sounds of a huge and vibrant student community. Change was in the air and the coffee bars and open spaces pulsated with conversation, music and dance. We felt privileged spectators and quite at peace. On one particular day as we watched an impromptu open air musical performance that brought delight to a gathering audience, I noticed an old man standing a little distance away from the crowd. He was carrying a placard proclaiming the words 'REPENT AND PREPARE'.

At the time he appeared an inoffensive if somewhat incongruous presence in such a celebratory atmosphere. He reminded me of similar prophets of doom of my youth, standing outside the football ground, stoically enduring banter or abuse from the crowd depending on the outcome of the game. In this instance, the assembly barely acknowledged him. There was too much going on and perhaps this was the latest of many such visits he made to the campus. He seemed undeterred by the lack of attention and, in a curious way, perhaps even dependent on it. He was a silent witness to scriptural verities that he clearly thought had some relevance on this sunniest of days. We were all enjoying ourselves but his task was to remind us that good times end, as indeed do our lives, and only the foolish or ungodly ignore the need to make ready for a final reckoning.

The best I could manage by way of response was a sort of silent nod in his direction that acknowledged his determination to be counted. I couldn't quite get him out of my head however and a week later I recalled the incident in a sermon to a nearby congregation. As I think about him now, several months later, it occurs to me that Carver would have enjoyed constructing a short story around him. His stories, like his poems, embrace evocative scenes and characters. They frequently pay homage to the eccentric and odd and find in both some sort of redeeming knowledge. He meditates on his subjects, rarely judges them and bequeaths instead a form of loving attention that is religious in its devotion.

In the story that I am now imagining, we follow our campus prophet back to his lodgings. His stint is over for today, with few or no conversions. A typical day's work really: redeeming the multitude is a slow business with many setbacks. There is no family to greet him as he returns to his cheap hostel room, just the usual cracked crockery on the table and walls festooned with Bible texts. There is no television and he spends the time gazing from his window, anxiously contemplating the passing souls he so desperately longs to save from the coming wrath. Evening falls and he picks at a meal from the microwave or a tin. More Bible study, before a time of prayer and rest in an unmade bed. Tomorrow and the day after will tend to the same pattern: a prophet must be consistent in the doing of the master's work. Tomorrow however turns out not to resemble the past, and goes against the grain of expectation. Some sort of intervention occurs – divine or human, who is to say? – that, far from ushering in the kingdom with cries of tribulation, sets this man on a new path. His road is now less stony, illumined as it is by a more kindly light. Something has happened.

Maybe a waitress murmurs a reassuring word as she pours his coffee in the local diner. Perhaps he notices for the first time the sight of a carefree child skipping at her parent's side or the threadbare customer at the nearby table taking massive pleasure in the ample breakfast that will sustain him through another day. It might just be the sight of an autumnal tree that now seems a thing of great and unexpected beauty. All we can say is that there has been a shift in his understanding and awareness. He seems more open and available to the world and to others. He still reads his Bible, but his mood is less apocalyptic. For the first time he is aware of passages that tell of blessing rather than curse. His placard disappears from the campus gatherings. He is seen conversing with others, wondering perhaps what is expected of him in this new dispensation. He smiles more than he used to and thinks often with gratitude of the moment that cleansed his vision and enabled him to see.

From my reading of Carver there are good reasons to suppose that he would endorse this story along with its affirmation of the world as a place of flourishing. He knew after all from personal experience that a man can begin a second life and discover the world anew. And without ever pointing the finger or resorting to exaggerated self-pity, he was able to acknowledge how we sometimes get things horribly wrong and stand in need of restoration. He recognised that beyond our compulsive drives and desires there is the bigger moral question of what we owe to each other as human beings in terms of civility, service and community, and what might be possible 'if the tiger is flushed from hiding'[8] and the world is seen in a different light:

In the very essence of poetry
there is something indecent:
a thing is brought forth which
we didn't know we had in us,
so we blink our eyes, as if
a tiger had sprung out
and stood in the light lashing his tail.

(Czeslaw Milosz, 'Ars Poetica?')

It would be a fine thing to relate at this point that fact and fiction converged following my brief campus encounter with the silent man standing close by on that most lovely of days. It would please me to know that his life had acquired a new circumference and that he was no longer troubled by the disapproving eye of God. As a matter of record, I never saw him again for the duration of our visit but the knowledge of his absence has, paradoxically, contrived to make his presence more deeply felt in these pages. I hope to return to Berkeley at some point and – to continue the story – I can see myself relaxing with him on the campus over coffee. I have given him a copy of Carver's poems and he is telling me where it went wrong before he blinked his eyes in disbelief as the tiger emerged from hiding.

He had misread the signs, always expecting a flood of biblical proportions to wash everything away or an earthquake that would fracture the earth beneath his feet. He had ignored or passed over the promise of God in scripture to set a rainbow in the sky as a seal that 'never again shall there be a flood to destroy the earth' (Gen. 9:11). He had forgotten (if indeed anyone had ever taught him) the ancient wisdom that God has no pleasure in the destruction of the living 'for he created all things that they might be, and he made the nations of the earth for health' (Wisd. 1:14). On sunny days when the heavens proclaimed the glory of God he had seen only that the times appeared evil and the people lost. From the figure of Christ he had taken too much to heart the message of self-denial and renunciation, without ever realising that the invitation to take up the cross and follow Jesus issued from One who also told us to delight in the flowers of the field and to see the good earth as a token of God's love. And on those countless evenings, as he had returned home and contemplated the vanity and self-seeking of so much human endeavour, his broodings never impressed upon him that notwithstanding their waywardness, human beings are also 'fearfully and wonderfully made' (Ps. 139:13) and exist to reflect the love that animates and upholds all things (Gen. 1:26–27). We may be dust to the bone, caught in the web of time and finally scattered on the wind, but we also know ourselves to be more than this, blessed as we are with the wound of conscience, a capacity for unceasing compassion and the innate curiosity that drives our search for knowledge and deeper understanding.

He is relaying all this to me in a measured rather than excited tone – it is after all some time now since a moment of transfiguration pointed him in a new direction. There is a pause, and, without prying into what exactly happened, I ask cautiously how the event changed him – the difference it made to his feelings concerning the beautiful, the good and the true. Another pause before he slowly speaks a sentence that tells me all I need to know: 'I stopped believing everything was wretched'.

This proves a moment of liberation for me, conscious as I am of the incalculable damage and hurt that the word 'wretched' has inflicted upon our religious sensibilities. It so happens that I am writing this opening chapter at the beginning of Lent, a season in which I pray daily the Collect for Ash Wednesday. It is a splendid prayer, at one level reminding us of God's great enduring goodness: 'you hate nothing you have made and forgive the sins of all those who are penitent'. The problem emerges later, towards the end of the Collect: 'create and make in us new and contrite hearts that lamenting our sins and acknowledging our wretchedness we may receive from you the God of all mercy perfect remission and forgiveness'.

The difficulty lies in the fact that I cannot bring myself to recite publicly, especially in the presence of my congregation, that the *only* irreducible and genuinely significant religious truth about ourselves concerns our wretchedness. The theology of the Collect is so skewed at this point concerning what it means to be truly human that I always substitute the word 'unworthiness' for 'wretchedness' and encourage my ministerial colleagues to do the same. This is not a matter of tinkering with the liturgy to render it more palatable by ironing out the hard bits that register our depravity. It is rather to assert and insist that wretchedness alone will simply not do as the moral and spiritual measure of what we are and might become. We are frequently unworthy as we zigzag our way through the 'wilderness of this world'[9], placing heavy burdens upon our backs and those of others. But this is not all that we are required to say in terms of our humanity. There is another fact about ourselves that has to be set alongside our stupidities, cruelties and contradictions; it fosters hope and all worthy ambition and ultimately enables us to join in redemption's song with real conviction. Our vocation is to become 'partakers of the divine nature' (2 Pet. 1:4). We are encouraged to aspire to this highest of callings because, in words of immense reassurance and promise, we are 'God's work of art' (Eph. 2:10) – partners with him in the continuing work of creation and redemption. Jewish wisdom describes this mutual task in terms of *tikkun olam*, the means whereby we try to repair what is broken in the world.

By contrast, part of the misery of Christianity has arisen out of its failure, or refusal, to view the world in a positive light. Too often it has expressed disdain for human appetites, contempt for earthly joys and simple pleasures, and condemnation of what is arguably one of the most engaging human traits – our capacity for curiosity and wonder. In its more baleful teachings, the Church has sometimes viewed this world as a worthless bauble, earthly life as a distraction from the world to come and the human heart as little more than a rag and bone shop of reckless desires. The theological concept of *curiositas*[10] has relevance here. It was originally formulated in order to condemn speculation and intrigue about the universe because they shifted concentration away from the more pressing spiritual tasks of sober living and holy dying that alone equipped the Christian for heaven:

> To pursue knowledge under the impetus of curiosity was indeed to be like Adam in the garden, and his knowledge was disastrous. Further, curiosity was related to instability, aimlessness, restlessness and so to wandering about. [11]

The irony of this passage is not lost on me. *Curiositas* was a charge occasionally levelled against pilgrims who were thought to be too frivolous on their journeys – seekers of novelty who lacked a truly penitential heart. It occurs to me that as part of the carefree assembly that had gathered on the Berkeley campus to laugh and make music and be at ease with each other, I had made a pilgrimage of sorts. I had travelled a great distance to a world renowned place of learning, creativity, cultural diversity and intellectual exploration. I had stood alongside others savouring the joy of the moment and the well-being and happiness of those around me. I had seen in their faces intimations of that goodness which asserts powerfully that this world is not dirty but blessed and that it is precisely here that we begin to experience the life and joy of heaven. For all this, I was in the estimation of mediaeval theologians a guilty man, preoccupied with the world at the expense of higher and more sacred mysteries. Thankfully, more nuanced teachings emerged later and a pilgrimage itinerary 'could combine with it an account of worldly exploration signalling a shift in motivation that was to distinguish the Renaissance voyager from the mediaeval pilgrim'[12].

Underpinning the stories and poems of this opening chapter, and, indeed, running through them, is the religious conviction that without sacrificing the concepts of sin or salvation that will be considered later, any talk of redemption is ruinous if it proceeds from the premise that human beings are basically wretched and the earth is a forsaken place. The facts point in the other direction. The world continues to exhibit a fascination and power of meaning for many people in the dust, duties and celebrations of daily life. It is not a place to be despised or rejected, and, in their experience of its beauty and unexpected disclosures, such people come to know the blessedness of God's ways and his love for all things made (Gen. 1:31). True religion therefore must learn to speak to people in their strengths, hopes and possibilities and not only as, sadly, too often happens, in their weakness, loss or the presumption of their wretchedness. It is possible that they will come to the beauty and truth of Christ later. It is enough for now to celebrate their capacity for joy, their readiness to 'kneel down in forest groves' or ask for help as the mist of a waterfall blows against their face. It is enough, in other words, to know that this is already a transfigured world: a place where people get it badly wrong yet begin again; a kingdom in the making that fuses earth with heaven and time with eternity; a sphere where, if we follow the poet, and look more carefully, a passing child, a local diner or nearby tree can become epiphanies and annunciations. The energy of God is everywhere[13] and the world is a theatre of his glory.[14]

Notes

[1] Raymond Carver, *A New Path to the Waterfall: Last Poems* (Collins Harvill, 1990).

[2] Carver, *A New Path*, p.14.

[3] Carver, *A New Path*, p.22.

[4] Carver, 'No Need', in *A New Path*, p.155.

[5] Carver, 'What the Doctor Said', in *A New Path*, p.149.

[6] Carver, 'The Toes', in *A New Path*, p.53.

[7] Carver, 'Sunday Night', in *A New Path*, p.87.

[8] Carver, *A New Path*, p.24.

[9] From the opening lines of John Bunyan's *The Pilgrim's Progress*, first published in 1678.

[10] The concept of *curiositas* was a feature of early mediaeval thought associated with such writers widely separated in time as Augustine, Bernard and Aquinas.

[11] J. G. Davies, *Pilgrimage Yesterday and Today: Why? Where? How?* (SCM Press Ltd, 1988), p.85.

[12] Davies, *Pilgrimage*, p.86.

[13] The Eastern Christian tradition sees the whole of creation filled with the energy of God. Basil the Great asserts: 'No one has ever seen the essence of God, but we believe in the essence because we experience the energy'. Quoted in Kallistos Ware, *The Orthodox Way* (Mowbray, 1979), p.27.

[14] John Calvin refers to the natural world as the *theatrum gloriae dei* – the sense of the holy in creation. John Calvin, *Institutio Christianae Religionis*, 1.xiv.20 and 11.vi.1.

CHAPTER 2

The Human Riddle

Recently I came across the strange and instructive tale of William Brodie, more commonly known by his eighteenth-century Scottish contemporaries as Deacon Brodie.[1] I knew nothing about him until his name appeared in a footnote of something else I was reading. I knew that I had to dig a little deeper and felt instinctively that he had something to contribute to the business of this book. So it proved.

Brodie was a person of some distinction in his home town of Edinburgh. He was a man who took part. By day he epitomised respectability, industriousness and civic pride. He was a cabinet maker, installing and repairing locks and security mechanisms, a city councillor and deacon (or president) of the local trades guild. He was called to jury service and moved in the charmed circles of the Edinburgh gentry that included the poet Robert Burns and the painter Sir Henry Raeburn. On the surface he appeared to the world an accomplished, successful and important person. By night, however, a different character emerged. Under the cover of darkness he became a burglar and thief. His daytime work gave him access to the homes of the rich and he was able to copy their security keys using wax impressions. His takings, accumulated over almost twenty years and aided by the recruitment of a gang of three thieves, financed his second life, including five children, two mistresses who had no knowledge of each other and a gambling habit.

His downfall came in 1786 when he bungled an armed raid. Initially evidence was hard to find until copied keys, a disguise and pistols were found in his house. At his trial, that began on 20 August 1788, the jury found Brodie guilty. He was hanged on 1 October, using a gallows he had designed and paid for a year earlier. One account of his death records that he wore a steel collar and silver tube to prevent the rope from being fatal. Another tale tells of the hangman being bribed to secure the quick removal of the body in the hope of reviving it. The more prosaic truth is that he was placed in an unmarked grave at the parish church in Buccleuch.[2] His notoriety and daring, however, ensured that his story continued. There were even rumours that he had been seen in Paris long after the execution. Almost seventy years later, a small, sickly boy by the name of Robert Louis Stevenson, who had spent much of his childhood in bed reading books, became aware of the story. In his room there was a cabinet that had been made by Brodie and the deeds of its maker fed his imagination. The divide between Brodie's respectable daytime facade and the nature of his nocturnal habits confirmed in the boy what he had already been taught in his disciplined Christian upbringing: there was a clear division between good and evil. Years later as a student, Stevenson freed himself from the strict morals of his parents. Born in Heriot Row in Edinburgh's New Town, the smart part of the city, he could now be found enjoying the seedy nightlife of the Old Town. Sometimes he assumed a false identity for his forays into this very different world, and it was here – in his mind and imagination – that another dichotomy emerged in the difference between the New Town and the Old Town. One city, breathing, so to speak, with two lungs that represented quite separate realities.

Stevenson continued to be fascinated by this idea of 'doubleness' that was evident in people and places. He wrote a play about Brodie, and the notion that we all contain a 'shadow', infinitely more complex and murkier than our public selves, found its way into one of the books that brought him fame as a writer.[3] In 1885, living with his wife in the quiet coastal town of Bournemouth in order to safeguard his health, he had a dream that would change his life and generate a legend that has fascinated and disturbed readers ever since. *Dr Jekyll and Mr Hyde* came to him in his sleep. He wrote the first draft of the book in three days. His wife disliked it so he burnt the manuscript and wrote a second, again in three days. After some rewriting it was published in January 1886 as a cheap 'shilling shocker', and was an immediate success. The story takes the age-old conflict between good and evil and gives it a new twist. Both alike are now to be found in the same person: Dr Jekyll lives close to Cavendish Square, London, an affluent centre of medicine and the home of doctors and surgeons. A few minutes walk from his grand house lies another world where ragged children, lost souls and criminals populate the landscape of the night. The Old and New towns of Stevenson's youth live again, now assuming fresh yet still divided identities. And Dr Jekyll, for all his urbane ways and circle of cultured gentlemen (the spirit of Deacon Brodie still hovers!), also houses the beast Hyde 'who is the essence of cruelty, malice and selfishness'[4]. Both characters are now part of our language. The story retains its potency and appeal through constant retelling on stage and screen. If the Hyde of legend is more of a beast than Stevenson originally intended – the transformation begins with the stage play of *Dr Jekyll and Mr Hyde* in London in 1888 as Jack the Ripper plies his gruesome trade in the impoverished streets of the East End – he lingers in our consciousness as a dangerous memory and reminder of our morally conflicted selves.

'Doubleness' sums up the state we are in. The human heart, properly understood, is a repository of light and lies. Deacon Brodie lives on through Stevenson's creations and their dramatic embodiment of the imperfection of our human nature.

A pause is called for here to explain why I am sharing these stories. Most obviously, they are compelling narratives that speak to our curiosity and imagination. I knew there was a connection between Brodie and Stevenson, but it was only by digging that my appreciation of a great book was enhanced. Increasingly, in this respect, I incline to the view that in relation to our spiritual growth, it's not *what* we look at but *how* we look at it that matters most. Once we know the background, *Jekyll and Hyde* becomes much more than a fable 'of great foolishness and mad ambition'[5]. It is a mirror of our own skewed preoccupations, our morally dodgy motives (even when we think we are doing good) and our ability to sour what is sweet through our inordinate desires.

This is the stuff of true religion as I have come to understand it – the attempt to speak imaginatively and honestly concerning our human predicament. We are emphatically 'a little lower than the angels' (Ps. 8:5) and if we shine less brightly it is because we constitute a twisted mystery. It seems that we are 'created half to rise and half to fall; great lord of all things, yet a prey to all'[6]. This is how things are with us and we should not be deceived.

Echoing the opening chapter, we are right to feel ourselves blessed as part of a creation that exists for our flourishing and bears the hallmarks of divine giftedness and grace. But we must also acknowledge the kind of creature we are: capable of the highest good on the one hand and, on the other, too readily disposed to squander the world's juice and joy.

Our 'doubleness' partly explains the restlessness we often experience at the dissatisfaction with ourselves that arises even in a time of plenty, the inability to feel entirely comfortable in our skin and the uninvited questions that surface from time to time concerning the ultimate meaning and worth of things. It is not only that we are rarely, if ever, completely happy[7]; it is also our keen awareness of a longing for some kind of inward peace or resolution and the sense that something fundamental within us needs to be fixed or addressed.

The poems and plays of T. S. Eliot chart this condition very well. Lines from his play *The Cocktail Party* have stayed with me for the better part of thirty years with their haunting awareness of a deep but unspecific failure 'Towards someone, or something, outside of myself' and the accompanying need to atone.[8]

Significantly, the feelings of inadequacy or regret and the need to make amends do not arise from any specific deed or action or the awareness of a particular fault within. They emerge instead from something more diffuse and intangible and point to a more basic refusal to honour or act on the best that is in us, the source of which lies beyond us yet, paradoxically, can often seem very near, occasionally overwhelmingly so. Few within the Christian tradition have described this experience better than St Augustine. Writing in the tenth book of his *Confessions*, and all too aware of the waywardness of his formative years, he recounts:

> Thou didst call louder and louder and didst break through my deafness.
> Thou didst shine radiantly and more radiantly and didst penetrate my blindness.
>
> Thou didst blow and I came to breath and life, and breathe in Thee.
> I did taste Thee, and I hunger and thirst after Thee.

This is the real thing – the compelling language of deep human longing and devotion, alerting us simultaneously to the consciousness of sin as a falling away from the light and the more gracious reality of One 'who is unmistakably real yet in the end indubitably elusive'[9]. I shall say more about this later. For now I want to return to my opening stories and the second reason for their inclusion here.

At one level they feed and illuminate, sometimes satisfying our questions concerning life's mysteries in a way that simple answers fail to match. But in pointing us to our internal contradictions – 'the two souls alas that dwell in my breast apart'[10] – they also demonstrate why the Christian message is still necessary and relevant in our time. It speaks to our need for redemption and seeks to respond to the questions implied in the contrariness of human existence. Consider: if no tensions or polarities existed within us; if there was no perceptible sense of 'doubleness' that makes us seem a moral conundrum; if no instances had ever been recorded, factually or otherwise, of the blindness, deceptions and deceits that led one of the most eminent philosophers of the twentieth century to speak of 'the crooked timber of humanity'[11]; there would be no place in the world for a gospel of redemption. There would be no moral evil or temptation from which we required deliverance, and no unsatisfied longings or desires to disturb us. In the absence of human frailty and mortal questions there would be no requirement to call upon the divine name or seek a rescue remedy in the form of a second Adam.

We have passed through such times before. I'm thinking here of the eighteenth-century Enlightenment and the words of the famous French mathematician and scientist, Pierre Simon Laplace.[12] Asked by Napoleon where God fitted in the universe he is reputedly to have replied: 'Sire, I have no need of that hypothesis'. To a religious sensibility it reads like a rather impudent one-liner of a man who has dispensed with faith in the service of reason and the natural sciences as the means whereby all human needs are addressed and all darkness dispelled. To a certain extent this was the case. There were many thinkers at the time who argued that it was necessary only to wait upon 'Mother Nature', or 'Dame Nature', for the guidance that combined with human ingenuity would build a better tomorrow. They were wrong. No student of history or the human heart believes any more in the Enlightenment myth of inevitable progress, or the risible idea that reason alone can address, let alone answer, the questions that have preoccupied some of the greatest minds for several millennia. The search for meaning abides and the cataclysms of the past century have left no room for facile optimism concerning the ability of nations or communities to live at peace one with another.

This much said, I still want to resist the stance that views the Enlightenment as nothing more than the enemy of Christianity, or an intellectual movement that sought to build a heavenly city on earth without recourse to God. If its assumptions concerning human perfectibility perished in the excesses and cruelties of the French Revolution that culminated in the reign of terror and the guillotine, we still need to ask why it was that creative and thoughtful minds had come to believe that reason rather than religion represented the best hope for humanity. The answer lies not only in the vast new realms of knowledge that were opening before them but in their championing of reason in an age of unthinking brutality and superstition. They were against ignorance, religious intolerance and the cruel absurdities of ecclesiastical authoritarianism that had made possible the rack and stake, the dungeon and the Inquisition. I have just one story to relate in order to make the point, but you will find it is enough.

As Pierre Simon Laplace moved towards adolescence and began to show the intellectual promise that would one day lead him to dismiss the deity and be compared to Isaac Newton as a scientist of the most eminent rank, Jean Calas, a shopkeeper from Toulouse, faced a personal crisis after forty years of quiet obscurity. One of his six children committed suicide after his ambition to become a lawyer had been thwarted on account of his Protestantism. A rumour began to spread that Jean Calas had murdered his son to prevent him from converting to Catholicism. Despite any real evidence, and Calas's unblemished life as father, husband and small businessman, he was sentenced to be tortured and killed. Accordingly, on 16 March 1762, he was tied between two rings and stretched until his four limbs were dislocated. He did not die and, with remarkable moral tenacity, continued to insist on his innocence. Sadly, for him, the next step entailed the *question extraordinaire* – the move from routine torture to the extraordinary questioning which involved increased brutality. Water was poured into his mouth until his body swelled to twice its normal size. Still unable to extract a confession, his torturers bound him to a scaffold, crushed his limbs and left him to die. Two hours later on discovering that he was still alive, they strangled him.

As this tragedy unfolded, the writer and philosopher Voltaire[13] was gaining a reputation as an implacable critic of the French Church and a champion of the oppressed. Learning of the Calas case, he spent three years clearing the dead man's name. After much letter writing and the publication of his *Treatise on Tolerance* he was successful in securing Calas's pardon. When he returned to Paris at the end of his life, he was venerated by the crowds as the 'preserver of the Calas'.

In the light of such awful misdemeanours sanctioned by religious authorities, it is not surprising that Voltaire became a hero to many. He was the person who above all others represented the light of reason 'whose light at last will flood the world'[14]. A touching sentiment in its way but one that failed to face all the facts concerning the desperate inability of humanity to consecrate reason, truth and imagination as the kindly lights that made possible the advance of knowledge and understanding. There was a darker narrative of human history that Voltaire acknowledged but he took no interest in it. His commitment was to the triumphs of reason and imagination, not their failures. He knew of barbarism and tyranny and accepted the necessity of cautionary tales to warn humanity of such horrors. But, in his elevation of reason to the highest throne, he failed to register the power of unreason – the furtive inner pattern that at best we see darkly and intermittently until it emerges into the light with furious effect, in the forms of war, repression, madness, anarchy and injustice.

The counter-blast to Voltaire came twenty years after his death and in the aftermath of the monsters born of the French revolution. His opponent, Joseph de Maistre[15], was to prove a formidable critic of the revolution and rationalism. His ordered world, predicated on Pope, King and God's providence, had been destroyed by what he had come to regard as a shallow and misguided view of life propounded by secular and enlightened thinkers. In response he wrote with passion, force and acuity concerning what he believed to be a truer estimation of basic human instincts and the Bedlam of a world created by humanity when it rejects the designs of the deity. Convinced to the core of his being that the philosophy of his day had perpetrated a terrible lie through its insistence that 'all is good', he insisted instead that evil taints everything and that human blood is always flowing somewhere on the globe. If reason leads to some human achievements it is the much deeper power of irrationality that eventually destroys. There is little by way of moderation in his style, but then he was a counter-revolutionary responding to a great calamity that had afflicted the common people and utterly resolved to discredit 'the rottenness that leads to nothing' – the intellectual and moral legacy of the Enlightenment. Here he is at his most uncompromising:

> Over all the numerous races of animals man is placed, and his destructive hand spares nothing that lives. He kills to obtain food and he kills to clothe himself; he kills to adorn himself; he kills in order to attack and he kills to defend himself; he kills to instruct himself and he kills to amuse himself; he kills to kill. Proud and terrible king, he wants everything and nothing resists him ... from the lamb he tears its guts and makes his harp resound ... from the wolf his most deadly tooth to polish his pretty works of art; from the elephant his tusks to make a toy for his child – his table is covered with corpses ...[16]

It is not a flattering portrait. Man is not only part of a wider nature that is red in tooth and claw. He is also ready 'at the first beat of the drum ... to go without resisting, often even with a kind of eagerness ... to blow to pieces on the field of battle his brother who has done him no wrong'[17]. Bafflingly, man also invents stories to make him weep and sheds tears for others. He can be compassionate and good yet he also desires wars and slaughter. He is a potential angel soiled with vice and (to use a modern term) forever *conflicted*:

> He does not know what he wants; he wants what he does not want; he does not want what he wants; he *wants* to *want*; he sees within himself something which is not himself, and which is stronger than himself. The wise man resists and cries 'who will deliver me?' The fool gives in and calls his weakness happiness.[18]

I find these passages fascinating, both in what they tell us about
Maistre and their view of human nature. They make it clear that
Maistre does not stand alone in his estimation of the world's ways.
He is resolutely a strand within a long Christian tradition and there
are echoes of St Paul, Augustine, Luther and Calvin in his rhetoric. If
we read that impassioned plea 'who will deliver me?' again we can
hear Paul wrestling with the same question (Rom. 7:24) as he too
contemplates the terrible ambivalence within himself, struggling to
choose between good and evil. Maistre inhabits the same kind of
universe and both are united in their belief that, notwithstanding the
spark of the divine spirit within us, we find it easy to dissipate our
energies upon futile or destructive ends and soon become feeble or
corrupt.

The extracts also raise the doctrine of original sin. Maistre
accepted this as the basis of his understanding of history and institu-
tions and the paradoxes of human existence. For him it shed light on
the human predicament and life's enigmas. We owe the doctrine
to St Augustine and, over the centuries, it has been criticised or
rejected for its illogicality, its fatalism and, most of all, its unfairness.
Even theologians have found its central affirmations preposterous or
contradictory. It is not helpful or encouraging to think of ourselves
as partakers of a ruined nature that is found in all people, is therefore
uniquely human and, from a Christian perspective, has its origins in
the disobedience of Adam (Gen. 3). Using the metaphors of medicine or genetics, the doctrine defines original sin as an infection or
infirmity, a virus transmitted from parents to children, like HIV, and
capable of being traced through successive generations to Adam, the
progenitor of the race. Luther spoke of the 'sickness of a nature
vitiated by sin'[19], and later Protestant confessions of faith[20] made
reference to the 'inborn disease'[21] that taints our nature. Things
become worse once we realise that Augustine saw the act of inter-
course as the means whereby sin was transmitted from one generation to another. As a consequence of his teaching, the procreative act
was regarded as intrinsically sinful, and a distorted view of human
sexuality defined the stance of the Church to the body.

Significantly (and, I want to add, encouragingly!) Augustine's
authoritative voice on the corruption of our nature, and its provenance in the story of the Fall recorded in Genesis 3, is also in some

respects a singular one. Judaism lacks a doctrine of original sin in its teachings. The prophets ignore Adam, Jesus himself never refers to the Adamic story, and, for Paul, Adam's fateful action is recorded only to illustrate the necessity of the saving work of Christ (Rom. 5:17–18). The temptation at this point (notice how the Fall retains its grip on our vocabulary!) is to put original sin to one side as an interesting but essentially flawed and incoherent doctrine that no longer has any purchase on our lives or imagination. To do this, however, would constitute a really big mistake, for, despite inconsistencies, this controversial teaching can still illuminate the riddle of our human darkness and 'account for the tangles and knots of experience'[22].

Part of the riddle – and to my surprise I find myself drawing here on the thought of Jean-Paul Sartre – lies in his observation that 'Man is a being to whom something happened'[23]. Not only does history contain frightening chapters that record 'the dreadful ambivalence of the distinctive privilege of being human'[24], it also reveals how human freedom can be turned towards evil and our wills corrupted. Human behaviour is sometimes 'out of order' and, following Sartre, we can only begin to make sense of this by asserting that, at some point along the way, something radically distorted our desire for the good. Various explanations have been put forward by thinkers as diverse as Marx, Freud and Hegel that interpret the plight of humanity as a species uniquely burdened as well as gifted and, in some sense, 'alienated' from a golden state or age. In each case the force and power of scriptural insight seems to touch their thinking and it is possible to see something like a primeval Fall in their writings.[25] The point is sufficiently made, I think: no account of human nature will do that fails to acknowledge the success of evil in our lives, how it has originated and why it is that each possibility for good we possess is accompanied by its opposite. In order to make some sense of existence, we need (and relish) the narratives, myths and stories that shed light on who and what we are.

A particular story told by Augustine relates to a day in his own life when he passed a beggar on the streets of Milan. He recalled the event vividly because the poor man was laughing and joking. Augustine was filled with sadness: his own life seemed to be on track and on that very day he had been writing a speech to be delivered to the emperor. He was surging with ambition and energy, fuelled by a desire for worldly success but also for inward peace. The smiling beggar, however, seemed to mirror his own inward state. The pauper's happiness was illusory – probably induced by drink or madness – and it suggested to Augustine that his own path was choked with weeds. He recognised that the road he had adopted was not straightforward and reflected much that was little better than posturing, preening, contrivance and manoeuvring – second-rate or selfish activities that could never lead to the simplicity and peace of the pure in heart. Like many other seekers after truth, he had come to know of the restless heart that could rest only in God and the sin that consumed the spiteful minutes of too many days.

Why was this? Augustine traced it to the human desire to be divine. In the story of the Fall, he saw that the original sin of Adam and Eve was repeated in the pride of every subsequent individual. By not relying on God, evil becomes possible and we are caught in a vicious spiral, out of control and often far removed from the civilisation of love. As we look around the world, we can hardly doubt that there is something powerful and profound in Augustine's analysis. The reality of original sin is confirmed by our actual experience of ourselves and others. In pointing to the fragility and waywardness of the human will, this ostensibly fierce doctrine is also strangely consoling, for it serves as a preamble to good news. It teaches us that to be human is to fail morally and that we need to be realistic about this fact.[26] It invites compassion and mercy, and urges us to think no worse of others than of ourselves. It reminds us that we are *all*, as we are by nature, *companions* in the divine and morally arduous business of being authentically alive.

The Enlightenment, as we saw earlier, took issue with such claims. If the lamp of reason shone into the dark corners of the world in order to expose cruelty, quackery and plain nonsense (and for these reasons I believe it deserves at least two cheers), it also denied original sin in its most perverse manifestations and asserted instead the freedom rather than the bondage of humanity. From a considerable distance we are now able to judge the competing arguments of Voltaire and Maistre, and the extent to which we are genuinely free and not like flies caught in a web. This is not a matter of deciding, in any final sense, who between them was right or wrong, but how they can help us to see more clearly into the riddle of our 'doubleness'. It is this fact about ourselves that leads us to rejoice and despair as we contemplate the ethical project of how we are to live. It is this fact alone that should be uppermost in our minds as we utter the Lord's Prayer and ask for deliverance in the name of One who is holy and strong, and whose nature contains all mercies.

Notes

1. Born 28 September 1741 – died 1 October 1788.
2. Brodie is commemorated by a pub named after him on Edinburgh's Royal Mile. In 1975 Forbes Bramble wrote *The Strange Case of Deacon Brodie* (publisher Hamish Hamilton) and in 1997 a television film of the same name featured Billy Connolly.
3. Stevenson wrote more than thirty books: novels, travel diaries, plays and collections of essays and stories, some of them in collaboration with other authors. His first full-length novel, *Treasure Island* (1883), brought him to the attention of the public.
4. R. L. Stevenson, *Dr Jekyll and Mr Hyde* (Dorling Kindersley, 1997), p. 62.
5. Stevenson, *Dr Jekyll,* p. 10.
6. Alexander Pope, English poet (1688–1744), *An Essay on Man,* Epistle 2.
7. Recently there has been a resurgence of interest in happiness, that has produced several academic studies. See R. Layard, *Happiness: Lessons from a New Science* (Penguin, 2005), and R. S. Schoch, *The Secrets of Happiness: Three Thousand Years of Searching for the Good Life* (Profile, 2006).
8. Cited in F. W. Dillistone, *The Christian Understanding of Atonement* (Nisbet, 1968), p. 1.
9. Rod Garner, *The Big Questions: Believing with Heart and Mind* (SPCK, 1995), p. 8.
10. Quotation from *Faust*, cited in Dillistone, p. 4.
11. Isaiah Berlin, *The Crooked Timber of Humanity: Chapters in the History of Ideas* (Vintage Books, 1992). The title of the book owes its origins to an earlier quotation of Immanuel Kant (1724–1804): 'Of the crooked timber of humanity was no straight thing ever made.'
12. Pierre Simon Laplace (1749–1827).
13. Voltaire (1694–1778), real name Francois-Marie Arouet.
14. Robert Greenwood, cited in J. Stangroom and J. Garvey (eds.) *The Great Philosophers* (Eagle Editions Limited, 2006), p. 67.

[15] Catholic scholar and philosopher born in 1753 in Chambery, part of the kingdom of Sardinia. Educated by Jesuits he became part of a lay order that gave help to criminals and comfort to the victims. He was devastated by the bloodshed of the French revolution.

[16] Part of *Soirees de Saint-Petersburg* cited by I. Berlin, *Crooked Timber*, p. 111.

[17] *Soirees,* v. 3–4.

[18] *Soirees,* iv. 67–8.

[19] Henri Blocher, *Original Sin; Illuminating the Riddle* (Apollos, 1997), p. 110.

[20] For e.g. The Augsburg Confession of Faith (1530), which elucidated essential Lutheran doctrines.

[21] Blocher, *Illuminating*, p. 110.

[22] Blocher, *Illuminating*, p. 84.

[23] J. P. Sartre, *Cahiers pour une Morale* (Paris, 1983), p. 51.

[24] Blocher, *Illuminating*, p. 90.

[25] 'Marx *did* share with the ancients a belief in a past Golden Age.' Cited by Gary North in Blocher, p. 101.

[26] ' "Know thyself?" if I knew myself, I'd run away.' Quotation of Goethe cited in Mark Vernon, *42: Deep Thought on Life, the Universe and Everything,* (OneWorld, 2008), p. 137.

CHAPTER 3

The Cross: for Us and for All Creation

We have cleared the ground a little. In these opening chapters, without, I hope, too much inconsistency or contradiction, we have placed our bets, so to speak, on a dual-theology that delights in the possibilities of human life and the created order without denying the 'doubleness' that defines us and thwarts our best aspirations. In the most ordinary lives there is much that is good that invites our compassion, respect and love, and points us to One who is always and everywhere present. Such gracious facts, however, do not allow us to set aside the knowledge of the darkness within ourselves that makes us dangerous and dissatisfied. To this knowledge we must also add our awareness of living in a world with 'ragged edges', where order and disorder are interwoven in such a way that we can be overwhelmed at any moment by calamity and dismayed by the weight of suffering around us. The religious imagination has responded to this human predicament with stories and allegories that tell of caged lives, immortal longings and mortal questions. Here are the opening lines of a classic – John Bunyan's *The Pilgrim's Progress*. As he makes his way through the temptations and confusions of this life, Christian comes to a certain place where he lies down to sleep:

> And as I slept, I dreamed a Dream.
> I dreamed, and behold I saw a man clothed with rags, standing in a certain place ...
> with a book in his hand and a great burden upon his back. I looked and saw him open the book ... and as he read,
> he wept and trembled, and not being able longer to contain,
> he broke out in a lamentable cry; saying,
> what shall I do?[1]

Christian is fallen man. The scriptures in his hand have convicted him of his sin and now he needs to know what he must do in order to be saved (Acts 16:30). He finds the answer to his question in the form of an arduous journey to the Celestial City. The road winds uphill all the way and there are fierce encounters and serious panics before he reaches his goal. But, as he travels, kindly Help comes to his aid, providing the respite and assistance that all pilgrims need from time to time. '*Then,* said he, *Give me thy hand*; so he gave him his hand, and he drew him out, and set him upon sound ground, and bid him go on his way.'[2]

The forebears of Bunyan's allegory are traceable to medieval visions, moralistic sermons and scriptural narratives that form a complex tapestry of redemption. In order to be saved we have to travel. There is the necessity of struggle, the inevitability of failure and the duty not to despair. If *The Pilgrim's Progress* leans too much towards a quest for the personal assurance of salvation (remember that he is fleeing a city soon to come under judgement) and a view of the world that fails to reflect its hidden travails, its tone is concrete, and urgent. In its insistence that suffering and darkness are integral to a life of discipleship that has a cruciform shape, it also calls vividly to mind 'the dangerous memory of the passion of Christ'[3]. As Christian and those who follow him face the river of terror that must be crossed before they can enter the city that is the New Jerusalem, they are sustained by the vision of a 'head that was crowned with thorns, and the face which was spat upon for me'[4].

It is this sacred head and face that primarily concerns us in this chapter and for one reason only. A gospel of redemption must have at its heart the compelling, strange and lonely figure expiring upon the cross for the sake of the world (John 3:16). This image, so venerated in Christian tradition and so powerfully at work in much of what we see and hear in our churches, makes us more than 'a people of the Book'. Our commitment is to the religion of the cross. When archaeologists excavate the sign of the cross in the desert sand they know they are standing on holy ground where once, and even more so now, believers across the world define themselves in relation to the crucified Christ and his bitter agony. Each offering of the Eucharist makes present the mystery of the cross as those present are mandated to 'Do this in remembrance of me' – to take bread and

wine and receive them as strange tokens of the passion of Jesus. We
trace his suffering in the stations of the cross, and in Holy Week we
sing with particular poignancy: 'Were you there when they crucified
my Lord?' This Negro spiritual was first sung by black slaves in the
southern states of America, who fastened upon the death and resurrection of Jesus because his suffering reflected their own tribulations
at the hands of callous owners. It is no coincidence that 'the man of
sorrows' continues to speak to those who have lost their freedom or
feel too keenly the world's injustice. In the same way, the preaching
of St Paul spoke most readily to the lives of the abandoned and
oppressed. As heart confronted heart, the crucified Christ became
their brother:

> We are afflicted in every way, but not crushed; perplexed, but
> not driven to despair; persecuted but not forsaken; struck
> down, but not destroyed; always carrying in the body the death
> of Jesus so that the life of Jesus may also be made visible in our
> bodies.
>
> For while we live, we are always being given up to death for
> Jesus' sake, so that the life of Jesus may be made visible in our
> mortal flesh. (2 Cor. 4:8–11).

Paul does not want us to be deceived. Discipleship is about cost – we
can expect hardship, distress or perils (Rom. 8:35), but none of
these things will finally separate us from the Son of God who loved
us and gave himself for us (Gal. 2:20). We can hear Bunyan in these
words, and, if our gaze is truly attentive, we can also glimpse in the
image of the crucified 'the deepest visible point of the divine self-
giving, which entered history at Bethlehem'[5] and has its origins in
heaven itself. Redemption begins long before the cross. It is dis-
closed in a secret birth forever associated with the cold manger of
Christmas and has its cosmic genesis in Christ who is the 'image of
the invisible God, the first born of all creation' (Col. 1:15). Extraor-
dinarily and fantastically, Christ as the *first born* has supremacy over
all creation. He is present in the cosmos from the beginning, since
'all things have been created through him and for him ... and in him
all things hold together' (Col. 1:16–17). As a work of reconciliation

(Col. 1:20), the blood of the cross opens our eyes to the mystery of God's being as One who is 'spent and drained in that sublime self-giving which is the ground and source and origin of the universe'[6].

Redemption is a complex and costly tapestry. As Bunyan recognised, it calls for our participation and commitment as travellers and seekers and sets before us the sacred mystery of Christ, who, in his faithfulness unto death, makes possible the healing of our human hurt. Many find this claim preposterous. Many more continue to walk by, uninterested and unmoved by the story of Good Friday, and others delight in deriding an image and a story that has inspired the greatest Western art and music. But for those who believe and are prepared to honour the dying Christ through their emulation of his self-giving, this marginal figure of first century Palestine becomes the source of their strength and life. In a way that cannot be easily articulated but is nevertheless deeply felt as a truth beyond contradiction, the cross becomes redemptive and, as the liturgy of Good Friday affirms, 'the tree of defeat became the tree of glory; and where life was lost, there life has been restored'.

This is the language of faith and devotion. It is the hard work of prayer and silence. It is the fruit of struggle and contemplation as year by year we return to the foot of the cross, conscious of our waywardness but also aware of our desire and need to become truly decent human beings. Over time, and sometimes in precious moments of unguarded illumination, we begin to see that in order to follow this important vocation the essential requirement is not to become more religious but to share more fully in the suffering of God in the life of the world. This is a morally strenuous requirement that goes beyond rationality and is bound up with the lure of mystery. Being redeemed does require us to hold on to our brains, but more than this it calls for the obedience of faith, the consent of the will and risk of imagination. It cannot be confined simply to the personal pursuit of being saved, of an 'old Adam' which needs in some sense to be put away or cast off, and its proper scope lies in the promise of a new heaven and a new earth of which, in his dying and rising, Christ is foretaste and pledge (1 Cor. 15:20–24).

The claim being made here is vast in its implications for the destiny of humankind and, for me, represents part of the disturbing attractiveness of the gospel – its concern and ability to address and illuminate the most fundamental questions that separate us from the rest of the created order. In relation to what we may hope for, concerning the human future in the sure knowledge of our eventual death, and also that of the sun upon which we depend, the cross points us to Christ who lived among us in Palestine in the reign of the Emperor Tiberius and was crucified under Pontius Pilate. Following his resurrection, this real life and real death in a relatively short space of time came to be seen and worshipped as the human face of God, and was followed as 'the way, and the truth and the life' (John 14:6). The real world of flesh and blood, of sin and tragedy, into which he entered as a child 'born of a woman' (Gal. 4:4), was no mere stage-set or backcloth for the specific redemption of individual souls by some benign extraterrestrial deity with little concern for the material order. As the suffering servant foretold by Isaiah (Chapter 53), Jesus died in order to subdue *all things* to his Father's rule. By definition, all things embrace all times and seasons, the ultimate sovereignty of Creator over creation and the restoration of history, nature and personal relations into one harmonious whole where sin, suffering and decay shall be no more.

To the perennial question 'What think you of this man?' (Mark 8:27) – this Christ who is 'infinitely greater than any institution claiming monopoly of his secrets'[7] – we are obliged to say that he does not come to us as an isolated spirit with no interest in the world's affairs except the business of rescuing a fallen race. His incarnation incorporates him into the world (John 1:10) and his presentation as a child in the Temple, 'in substance of our mortal nature'[8], aligns him with all that is palpably human. His ministry on earth of healing, preaching and serving relates him to a kingdom that is bound up with the world's future. His saving work extends backwards and forwards, for 'as all die in Adam, so all will be made alive in Christ' (1 Cor. 15:22). Once again, *all things* constitute the aim and scope of divine restoration and alert us to the deep, hidden intention at the heart of the created order.

As a narrative of our comings and goings, and the grounds of our hope in a world where we often seem to be 'moving in a fog, uncertain of where we are heading'[9], this rich gospel of redemption speaks persuasively of the transcendent power of God that is at work in creation and is revealed so poignantly in a love that bears and endures all things (1 Cor. 13:7), even death on a cross. It remains a compelling vision, all the more so once we allow ourselves even a momentary awareness of the vastness of the universe in time as well as space and the complex processes that have led to life as we know it. Whatever redemption has meant or continues to mean in relation to the cosmic Christ that we have identified in the likeness of Jesus of Nazareth and his sacrifice, his saving work has to be set against the 'epic of evolution' – our ordered creation unfolding over billions of years with much evidence of regression, catastrophe and waste along the way. We can put this in the form of a question: if Christ crucified is both the true manifestation of who and what God is, and the apogee and source of all things (Col. 1 again), how are we to relate his cross to the whole sweep and development of a natural order that can leave us breathless with the constancy of its governing laws, and bewildered and sometimes broken by its earthquakes, floods and cancers?

A long and difficult question, admittedly, but one that sits well with New Testament teachings concerning the role and person of Christ and what we now profess to know about the origin of the universe, from the 'hot big bang' to the emergence of *Homo Sapiens* on earth. A belief in divine creation and the self-expression of God in the suffering and death of his Son 'has to come to terms with and, better, be integrated with and informed by scientific perceptions of the way in which life, including that of humanity, has come into existence'[10]. It is a matter of correlation – of relating faith to the world as it is in all its complex and precarious activity – that is best defined as a *creatio continua*. Creation is never still: we witness an inexorable biological drive to survive at every level that brings success and failure, death that bears much fruit from one generation to the next and a striving that confirms the wisdom of St Paul: 'the whole creation has been groaning in labour pains until now' (Rom. 8:22). In following the Psalmist, and extending Paul's metaphor, life is lived in green pastures and in the valley of the shadow of death. The close proximity of failure accompanies each little life and nature must reproduce or face extinction. The facts are that something is always dying, and something is always living on. There is no need to resist Darwin's celebrated and clinical conclusion here. If life on earth contains much that is beautiful, it is not Eden. Examined at closer quarters, it resembles a great amphitheatre where life clashes with life in the struggle to survive. Things perish in order that others may live, and biblical images abound. In the sacrifice of unsuspecting and innocent creatures may be glimpsed the slaughter of the inno-cents demanded by Herod following the birth of Christ or the apocalyptic image of the innocent lamb slain from the foundation of the world (Rev. 13:8). Struggling creatures are delivered over to death and, in the incompleteness and pathos of their lives, it is not sentimental to see something of the labour of divinity. Nature has a cruciform shape. In order to bring forth or give birth to the many creatures that will fill the earth (Gen. 1), the earth is always in travail. Before the long and laborious process that gives rise to consciousness and the dawn of humans, the path that comes out of Eden appears to the sensitive religious mind a *via dolorosa*. The shadow of the cross falls across the halting story of the earth and, until the resolution of all things in God, remains an adjunct of the temporal future.

An orthodox faith at home with scripture will not be surprised or necessarily alarmed by such disquieting truths. To be chosen or upheld by God is not to be spared adversity. The tragic history of Israel has come to represent the severest of covenants with God, bearing out the etymology of the name Israel as 'a limping people'. One of its own – a son of Abraham and an urgent proclaimer of the kingdom of God, also testified to the necessity of the suffering that would mark his own human journey and the lives of those who embraced it in the hope of a greater freedom. As the divine son, he submitted to spite, hatred, idle curiosity and death 'on a squat hill top by Jerusalem'[11]. The symbol of this cross – too often misunder-stood as only and ever a payment to the Father for the price of sin or the rescuing of human souls – stands for something altogether greater that binds the cross to the whole of creation. The atonement of Christ is all-embracing: his cross is nature's sign as well as ours, and it serves as a parable of a shared history defined by a never ending pattern of struggle, dying and rising. Earth's story is a passion play long before Gethsemane and Golgatha, and its forms and flourish-ings are always bought with a price:

> Every organism is plugged into a struggle in which goodness is
> given only as it is fought for. Every life is chastened and
> christened, straitened and baptised in struggle. Everywhere
> there is vicarious suffering. The global Earth is a land of
> promise, and yet one that has to be died for ... Since the
> beginning, the myriad creatures have been giving up their lives
> as a ransom for man. In that sense, Jesus is not the exception to
> the natural order, but a chief exemplification of it.[12]

If we hold this last sentence for a moment and allow its proper
theological significance to register, what is being argued for here is
not a vision of nature locked in permanent struggle, with no end but
the unceasing conflict of tooth and claw. Something deeper is at
work: the eye of knowing faith enables us to view the emergence and
growth of the natural order as an upward road or climb[13] towards
the Omega Point[14] that is Christ. The immense labour of creation
over time has produced suffering and failure, tears and blood, along
the way. But something else is observable that is no less remarkable,
and represents a truth that is on the side of life. There also is evidence
of creativity, increasing complexity, the emergence of consciousness, ordered patterns of behaviour, and moral intuitions that extend
beyond self-preservation or that of a species and lead us into the
realm of sacrifice as the highest good. The agitation and friction of
life opens on to a road which has a direction and orientation, for on
its crest is placed the cross. We are called not to succumb to the
shadows but to climb in its light. In its features we find not only the
tragic depredations of nature but also the intimation of a glory that is
still to be revealed (Rom. 8:18). The love that seemed to have been
lost and given over to death comes flooding back out of the darkness
with a new and indestructible pattern surpassing even the dominion
of death.

There is much that has been left unsaid in this chapter – little or
nothing about the cross as an offering to an aggrieved Father, or a
ransom for sin, or a debt to the devil. In this respect, as a theologian
and teacher, I am conscious of how much has been written on these
controlling themes or images within the Christian tradition. There
are many interpretations of the cross and theories of atonement seek
to give objective weight to the saving work of Christ. All of them are

open to question on moral, theological or philosophical grounds. Sensitive minds within and beyond the Church find the notion of an implacable Father punishing his Son for the sins of the world morally offensive. And, to sceptical or cynical minds, the frequent claim that to be religious is to have been born again is denied by the outward evidence. As one of Christianity's fiercest critics noted: 'Show me you have been redeemed and I will believe in your Redeemer'[15].

For myself, I remain content to live with the mystery of the cross, and not just because I find the traditional theories concerning its significance unsatisfactory or limiting. When I first began the study of theology more than thirty years ago, I wrote in a journal the following words of John Henry Newman: 'How Christ's death brought about our salvation will ever be a mystery in this life'[16]. The long passage of time and the deepest events of my life and ministry at a personal and pastoral level have not altered my view that these are wise words. The crucified Christ cannot be confined to any one theory or doctrine, or, for that matter, a self-absorbed quest for personal assurance in the knowledge of our sin or fear of being condemned. I have suggested here, however inadequately, that his death is a moment in history that opens up for us new possibilities of existence and a deeper understanding of the created order with all its hurts and sorrows. As Bunyan's pilgrim invites us to make the arduous journey that leads to a fuller life, he fails to notice that the uphill road we must travel also reflects the upward struggle of all living things set down in these pages. It is the sweep of life contained in that momentous phrase 'the epic of evolution' that requires (even *demands*, from a New Testament perspective) to be set within the saving act of One who gives himself to the creation through love. He asks us to do likewise, to take pains with the world and to choose the cinder path.[17] Ahead of us he sets a signpost, a tree of terrible heat whose flame consumes all that is demonic or cruel and whose ultimate fire invites our allegiance. The cross is not an answer to how the world is redeemed but an invitation to share in its suffering. Redemption entails surrender and the attention that is best described as prayer:

Philosophers have measur'd mountains,
Fathom'd the depths of seas, of states, and kings,
Walk'd with a staff to heav'n, and traced fountains:
But there are two vast, spacious things,
The which to measure it doth more behove:
Yet few there are that sound them; Sin and Love.

Who would know Sin, let him repair
Unto Mount Olivet; there shall he see
A man so wrung with pains, that all his hair,
His skin, his garments bloody be,
Sin is that press and vice, which forceth pain
To hunt his cruel food through ev'ry vein.

Who knows not Love, let him assay
And taste that juice, which on the cross a pike
Did set again abroach; then let him say
If ever he did taste the like.
Love is that liquor sweet and most divine,
Which my God feels as blood; but I as wine.[18]

Notes

[1] *The Pilgrim's Progress* was an instant success when it was first published in 1678. It was reprinted almost immediately and sold over a hundred thousand copies.

[2] *The Pilgrim's Progress* (Ward Lock & Company Limited), p. 15.

[3] Quotation of the liberation theologian, J. B. Metz, cited by Kenneth Leech in *We Preach Christ Crucified* (Darton, Longman and Todd, 2006), pp. 3–4.

[4] *The Pilgrim's Progress*, p. 254.

[5] Michael Ramsey, *The Gospel and the Catholic Church*, p. 25, quoted in Douglas Dales, *Glory Descending: Michael Ramsey and his Writings* (Canterbury Press, 2005), pp. 36–7.

[6] W. H. Vanstone, *Love's Endeavour, Love's Expense: The Response of Being to the Love of God* (Darton, Longman and Todd, 1977), p. 62.

[7] Donald MacKinnon, *Explorations in Theology* (SCM Press, 1979), p. 10.

[8] Part of Gospel Acclamation for Eucharist of Candlemass (Mowbray & Church House Publishing, 1991), p. 274.

[9] A description of Man in Milan Kundera's *Testaments Betrayed* (Faber & Faber, 2004).

[10] A. Peacocke, 'The Cost of New Life', in J. Polkinghorne (ed.), *The Work of Love: Creation as Kenosis* (Eerdmans Publishing/SPCK, 2001) p. 21.

[11] From the poem *The Killing of Edwin Muir*.

[12] Holmes Rolston III, 'Kenosis and Nature', in Polkinghorne, *Work of Love*, p. 60.

[13] 'There is a creative up-flow of life transmitted across a long continuing turnover of kinds, across a natural history that includes a struggle resulting in more diverse and more complex form of life. This whole evolutionary up-slope is a calling in which renewed life comes by blasting the old. Life is gathered up in the midst of its throes, a blessed tragedy, lived in grace through a besetting storm.' Rolston III, 'Kenosis and Nature', p. 59.

[14] A term first formulated by the French Jesuit priest and palaeontologist Teilhard de Chardin.

[15] Friedrich Nietzsche (1844–1900), German philosopher and critic.

[16] Cardinal John Henry Newman (1801–90), English theologian and poet.

[17] An image taken from Andrew Motion's collection of poems, *The Cinder Path* (Faber & Faber, 2009), p. 31.

[18] Poem 'The Agony', George Herbert, *The Complete English Works* (Everyman's Library, 1995), p. 34.

CHAPTER 4

Nothing Wasted? The Use of Suffering

The Christian pilgrim has a cross-shaped faith and is called to share in the suffering of Christ. From a worldly point of view, this mandate, derived in part from the previous chapter, is not the most inviting or consoling mission statement and, frankly, runs counter to our basic intuitions that are geared to self-preservation and the avoidance of pain. But the New Testament does not equivocate: writing to a scattered community of believers in the five provinces of Asia Minor whose faith is proving a costly undertaking, the apostle Peter, or a disciple writing in the name of the revered apostle, reminds them that they should 'not be surprised at the fiery ordeal' that has come upon them (1 Pet. 4:12). This is a temporary testing of their faith so that it may be found to be 'more precious than gold' (1 Pet. 1:7), but more than this it represents the pattern of suffering of One who was innocent and suffered unjustly for the sake of others. They have been left a divine example and should be ready to 'follow in his steps' (1 Pet. 2:21). Because Jesus had been exposed to similar tribulations, the believers are urged to learn from their experience in the belief that hardships can be educative. Here, as elsewhere in the New Testament, without subscribing to the morally repugnant view that sufferings are sent deliberately to try individuals, can be found a form of wisdom which affirms that the school of adversity is potentially conducive to spiritual growth: which can, in other words, prove redemptive. Individuals and communities can, and do, learn more about themselves and their possibilities in a time of pestilence, and may even in some instances be moved to a deeper awareness of the paradoxical nature of the love of God. These two claims form the substance of the following pages. Before going further, however, I want to lodge two important caveats.

First, not all suffering is redemptive and sometimes there is no persuasive answer to the problem of needless pain or its baffling meaninglessness. Religious triumphalism has no place on this tormented ground, and silence may be the only fitting response to situations that seem to deny the existence of divine justice or compassion. In the aftermath of the Holocaust, some Jewish theologians abandoned all forms of theological discourse that sought to give a meaning to the death camps and resorted instead to a text hallowed by their tradition: 'And Aaron was silent' (Lev. 10:3). Words, either written or spoken, should never knowingly trivialise instances of human tragedy that leave faith, hope and courage broken or destroyed.

Second, we should give no room, theologically speaking, to the perverse and distorted elements within Christianity that have sought to wallow in the wounds of Christ in a way that now seems morbid and masochistic. Bad religion can fixate on the blood of Jesus. In the thirteenth century, Mechtild von Hackeborn rolled over broken glass she had placed on her bed 'until her whole body dripped with blood so that she could neither sit nor lie down because of the pain'[1]. As a corrective to such misplaced devotion, Lucy Winkett notes in her recent book[2] that the woman afflicted with haemorrhages in the gospels (Luke 8:43–48) found that on touching the hem of Jesus' garment her bleeding did not grow worse but stopped. Exaggerated or harmful forms of asceticism generally lead to needless misery; by contrast, the story of a woman made whole refutes in the best way possible the mistaken notion that the exclusive concern of discipleship entails the seeking and embracing of pain. The art of living, expressed as both a human and a Christian ideal, is against the pursuit of suffering. It is for the more important business of what it means to be alive rather than prematurely dead, and how we might learn and even profit from the disappointments and griefs that are woven inextricably into existence. There can be no fulfilled or genuinely happy life without confrontation, at some point, of the trials or tragedies that we have not sought. In the two stories that follow are contained, so I have come to believe, the wisdom that sees unimagined and redemptive possibilities in the most unpromising situations. If these narratives fail to fit into the neat religious categories that are increasingly demanded by some believers in an age that has a questionable urge for certainties in matters of faith, they do, in my view, address our wounds and how they might be healed.

We begin in France with the life of Marcel Proust, writer and critic and author of the extraordinary novel *Remembrance of Things Past*, published in seven parts between 1913 and 1927. Born in 1871 near Paris, Proust was the son of a prominent doctor and a wealthy Jewish mother. He suffered with asthma from his early years, was a semi-invalid for most of his life and a virtual recluse well before the end of it. Notwithstanding such limitations he managed military service, studied law and literature at the famous Sorbonne in Paris, became a kind and generous friend to many and was to be seen in desirable restaurants, tipping generously and wearing the fur coat that accompanied all his social engagements. He had a near-miraculous understanding of others and knew what was in their heart. This knowledge did not always console him, for he was able to discern that behind kind words often lie the ulterior motives that call into question the elevated claims we make for friendship. He died aged 51, catching a chill after a party where companions noticed he was wearing three coats and two blankets. Bronchitis led to pneumonia and a burst abscess in his lung. The grilled sole he had ordered earlier remained untouched. Four months before his death, a newspaper had invited him to respond to the question: 'What would you do in the last hour of your life in the certain knowledge that it was to end as a result of a great cataclysm about to destroy a huge part of the continent?' His reply suggested that a trip to the Louvre or India might be a good thing in the circumstances, or a declaration of love to the object of one's hidden longings. In the face of imminent death, however, he was also of the view that readers should wake from their slumbers and recognise that life is a graced affair and that many ideas, studies, plans and projects are routinely postponed because we fail to register that 'we are humans, and that death may come this evening'.

In a quite fundamental way, Proust had been thinking about this question long before the newspaper solicited his reply. Up to his death, he had toiled at the seven volumes of his literary masterpiece that represented his search for truth. Under the guise of fiction, he recreated his life in sentences of great length and beauty that led other accomplished writers to believe their own efforts were mere scribble by comparison.[3] His preoccupations were obvious: the corrosion of time, its irreversibility and how we might stop wasting and therefore begin valuing its gifts and challenges. If his genius made him an assured chronicler of his past, his physical and psychological suffering deepened his insights and fostered his creativity.

Pain comes in many guises, some more evident than others. Proust is a fascinating and touching example of one for whom the landscape of his interior life was as fraught with difficulties as his outward existence. The details are important here. This is a man who spent the last fourteen years of his life in a narrow bed in a room where all superfluous noise was eradicated and a novel was written that led reviewers to compare its author to Shakespeare. In early life he had suffered the obsessive concerns of his mother, a skewed relationship that continued well into his adult years. She remained anxious about how well he was sleeping, and the evidence suggests that what she desired most was a patient rather than a son. She succeeded in this aim: Proust was gay and proved inept and clumsy in love's ways. There were crushes and brief encounters but nothing solid or lasting. Friends lavished false praise on his work without having bothered to read it. And some went so far as to suggest that his illnesses were rather overdone and amounted to a form of indulgence. Were they right?

Certainly Proust was of a delicate disposition. Even a glass of water before bedtime could lead to crippling stomach pains. Against such fragility, however, needs to be set the serious ailments that beset him. Asthma attacks continued all his life, the fits lasting over an hour and sometimes occurring as many as ten times a day. He could not even venture out in the summer, his windows were kept permanently shut and fresh air became an enemy. He was always cold and wore an overcoat and four jumpers if he had to leave the house. He travelled badly, coughed frequently, ate sparingly – eventually just one meal a day – could not abide noise and often had colds. In one letter to a friend he mentioned that, in the writing of a three-page correspondence, he had wiped his nose 83 times. In the long twilight years he became preoccupied with his own death and described his condition as 'suspended between caffeine, aspirin, asthma, angina pectoris and altogether between life and death every six days out of seven'.

We may be inclined to dismiss some of this, as some clearly did, as hypochondria. Friends urged him to take more sun and air and to distance himself from his physical afflictions. Presumably they were surprised, embarrassed even, when he slipped away at a relatively early age. Perhaps they had also failed to notice that pain is relative to the sufferer – what counts as a mild inconvenience to one person is a hammer blow to another. And quite likely they had forgotten (if indeed they ever knew) that this tiresome author, given to frequent complaints concerning his condition, as a young man had been subjected to a prolonged and painful operation to cure his asthma. Afterwards, at the first sight of a lilac in bloom, he was assaulted by a violent attack of asthma that turned his hands and feet purple and led others to fear for his life.

By now, even with this briefest of sketches, we may already be forming an opinion of this man. I am suggesting that we do not rush to criticise but recognise instead that in this instance we have a genuine example of a genius who made something out of his suffering. His presumed excesses become intelligible (and therefore forgivable) in the light of his early experiences, and, through the prism of his pain, he is able to offer us a way of negotiating and interpreting our own unhappiness and misfortunes that removes at least part of their sting. So how does he do this? If we think again for a moment of his earlier reflection, concerning the way in which the sure knowledge of our death should concentrate our minds and make us aware of the plans and dreams that we routinely abandon out of laziness or the mistaken notion that dying is something that happens to other people, we are reminded of the importance of the present moment and its power to heal and re-orientate our lives. In 'looking well' to this day, we can invest our best energies in its unfolding and in so doing make amends for 'time lost' (itself a very 'Proustian' concern). An old hymn gets this perspective exactly right:

> Redeem thy mis-spent time that's passed,
> And live this day as if thy last,
> Improve thy talent with due care;
> For the great day thyself prepare.[4]

Proust was not exercised overmuch by religious notions of an End Time or Judgement Day, but it is possible to glimpse in his writings an incognito Christ, who summons us to consider the lilies of the field and to sit lightly to the cares of tomorrow (Matt. 6:28–34). The requirement is that we should try instead to shape our hours, experience and awareness in such a way that we recognise the untried and unexpected opportunities that exist beneath the surface of today's troubling things (Matt. 6:34). This amounts to more than the realisation that suffering can build character. St Paul is our guide here, with his insistence that 'suffering produces endurance, and endurance produces character, and character produces hope' (Rom. 5:3–4). Proust, by contrast, is interested in the way in which pain opens up possibilities for intelligent or imaginative enquiry which are frequently overlooked or declined. In his view, we don't actually learn anything properly until a problem surfaces or we fall prey to thwarted intentions. Infirmity or deprivation of any kind makes us pay attention and learn; we engage with processes and experiences we would otherwise know nothing of or care about. If we sleep soundly and well until the alarm awakens, we shall never discover anything about sleep or even know that we are asleep. A bout of insomnia, however, or the need to attend a crying child in the night, is not without value. Both help us to appreciate and understand the mystery of sleep 'by throwing a light upon the darkness'. By feeling things in a different way (that is to say, painfully) we acquire new knowledge. A damaged ankle tells us about the body's weight and how it is distributed; rejection by a lover introduces us not only to heartache but the raw and frightening mechanisms of emotional dependency. There is a practical wisdom here that cannot be taught but only discovered by ourselves on a path that no one else can take for us. Personal griefs and sorrows contribute to our understanding of what it means to be authentically alive in the occasional and sometimes frequent harshness of the here and now.

Proust bears many burdens – his lover dies in a plane crash off the coast of Antibes – yet his writings illuminate and console because of their costly veracity. His truths are bought with a price and are bound up with his refusal to endorse the ignorance, denial or easy contentment that rarely see beneath the skin of things or tell us anything significant about the art of living. Some of the characters in his novel represent those we might call *wasteful sufferers*, foolish souls who have lost in love, been turned away from exclusive parties or tormented by fears of intellectual inadequacy or social inferiority. They suffer but they do not learn from such experiences, and resort instead to the predictable defence mechanisms which foster arrogance and delusion, indifference and rage. No insights are gained from their wounded natures, no attempt is made on their behalf to understand what lies at the root of their discontent. Madame Verdurin, for example, is the leading light of a salon that meets to discuss arts and politics. She is passionate about the former and succumbs to headaches when the beauty of music overwhelms her. Once, we are told, she dislocated her jaw by laughing too much. Her overriding concern as an aspiring socialite, bent on climbing the ladder of recognition, is that she is not on the invitation list of the most renowned aristocratic families and she desperately wants to be. She masks her disappointment and frustration by a proffered indifference – anyone who fails to invite her is simply 'a bore'. Inwardly, she is crumpled to the point of disintegration. Her sense of what is valuable is characterised by what she lacks – an invitation to the inner circle – and her fate is to condemn as tedious or common what she lacks, for no other reason than she lacks it. How much better and honest if she could only accept that there are always more people who don't invite us than do, or begin to understand the protocols and differences that exclude people from particular social circles. Then she could begin to learn and redeem her quiet desperation by facing the facts and making more positive responses.[5] Her problem, and hence the source of her pain, is the 'one-dimensionality' of her seeing. She registers only the surface of what she sees in a particular moment – the absence of an invitation that would otherwise enhance her self-esteem and further her long-term plan to rise in her social world. She needs instead to take time with what she sees, and to reflect upon it in order to grasp that what is actually in front of her is not just the surface but an indication of a wider state of affairs, bound up with issues of class, culture, celebrity, rank and privilege that constitute in coded form her best chance of a genuine rather than feigned contentment. In a recent address to the Church of England General Synod, Rowan Williams has described this exacting but morally necessary approach in terms of a 'three-dimensional way of seeing' that opens 'the ability to learn from each other' and recognises that 'we can't see everything at once'[6]. Had he been alive and well enough to attend, and sufficiently warmed by his many over-coats and jumpers, Proust would have found the strength to register his approval of the Archbishop's words. Removed in time from the confines of an ecclesiastical debating chamber, and rooted fitfully in age beset by its own particular rifts and prejudices[7], he had come to understand in his own way that seeing in three dimensions stops us wasting our time when it comes to 'filling in what remains of the diary'[8].

Proust's 'mission', if we can put it that way, is at once human and humane. He wants us to fulfil ourselves, to grasp that life as a project assumes the dimension of a vocation that should not be destabilised or needlessly impaired through our lack of vision or insight. Obstacles can contribute to our development, and he encourages us to see beyond our own agenda in order to recognise the illuminating minutiae of the familiar yet strange continuum we call the present. He is a wise man and, if we allow ourselves to be more radical or generous in our understanding of the Christian way, he can also take us into the realm of religion as the sphere in which we learn more of the truth of ourselves and the responsibility we bear as the principal agents of our success or failure.[9]

Our first story ends here but I promised you another. The second entails a return to Paris, this time to the early years of the previous century and the birth of another remarkable writer and intellectual who, like Proust, experienced deep afflictions, yet found within them not only an educative power but also a road to Christ. Simone Weil was born on 3 February 1909, into a prosperous, loving and demanding family of secular Parisian Jews. Her father was a doctor, a small, handsome and generous man, capable of disarming frankness yet easily wounded by the remarks of others. Madame Weil was also generous and blessed with a passion for life and a desire that Simone and her older brother Andre should receive the best education possible in order to realise their talents. Both children were prodigies: their childhood games consisted of memorising long passages from Racine, conversing in ancient Greek and solving problems in differential calculus. Not exactly conventional pastimes for the early years of life, but each set within a home and atmosphere that breathed tenderness and humour along with the highest expectations. Simone became a student and disciple of the philosopher

Alain[10] and attended the elite École Normale, where she eventually
became a professor of philosophy who devoted her life to the search
for truth and the cause of the poor and oppressed. She was a French
Jew who broke away from Judaism and became fascinated by the
mystery and beauty of Catholicism. Much as she came to love its
worship and explore the tenets of its faith, she was never baptised.
She felt that it was the will of God that there should be some men and
women who gave themselves to Christ without embracing the
religious establishment. As a matter of principle, and after much
reflection, she remained outside the Church in order to 'serve God
and the Christian faith in the realm of the intelligence'[11]. In her short
life – she died, aged 34, in England where she had planned to be sent
behind enemy lines as part of her support of the French Resistance –
she frequently found herself at odds with those in authority and
surprised her intellectual contemporaries by working in industry,
fields and vineyards and siding with the unemployed. In time, some
came to regard her as a saint, the patron saint of 'outsiders', who
brought about her death by refusing to eat more than the rations
allotted to the French soldiers and citizens who remained in her
native land. Others questioned her mental health and the obstinacy
of her search for purity. No one description is capable of capturing
her life or work, but to read her essays and correspondence[12] is to
struck by a rare and searching intelligence, a deep sympathy for the
suffering of others and the prevalence of pain in a fiercely singular
and committed life that always remained close to the dangerous edge
of things. Her pain can be understood in three ways. As a campaigner
who worked unceasingly for the foundation of a new and more
humane order, she had to live with the awareness that brute power
often overcomes the claims of justice and that many lives are disfig-
ured by oppressive structures and ideologies. Her decision to work
in a factory arose initially from a desire to be alongside those at the
bottom of the pile. But, as a slice of the 'real life' that she craved, it
exposed her to the burdens of others who lacked a voice or influence. She had known beforehand that there was suffering in the
world but as she laboured through long hours, or waited with others
at factory gates for work or went without food, she felt intensely the
pain of 'those who *do not count* – in any situation – in anyone's
eyes ... and who will never count'[13]. She also experienced political

disillusionment and the loss of so many hopes as war with Germany became more inevitable. Her poor health was another key factor. From the age of 20, she suffered from violent headaches that left her exhausted and fearful that she had a brain tumour. Her commitment to justice meant that she often neglected her bodily needs (food in particular), and persistent head pains made her eat even less. If at times she felt overwhelmed, she never gave in. She was not prepared to die without having first existed, and her suffering became a creative act. It was the means whereby she encountered a truth of existence: affliction existed in the world and she believed that 'one must share in it so as to understand how one can really remedy it'[14]. Now, as then, some will regard this as a wrong-headed form of martyrdom – suffering sought for dubious or misguided ends. A more nuanced view, however, will see in Weil a hunger for righteous-ness, a concern for the poor and the downright strangeness and clear-sightedness that bear the hallmark of prophetic witness. She was not for easy compromises or soft words and neither was she mad, self-seeking or wholly perverse. Evasions of any kind were a lie and she had something of what Martin Luther King called the 'creatively maladjusted' about her.

At a deep level, she remained in love with the world. Its beauty represented 'its truly precious things' and appeared to her in a sacramental light. Reading her again after some years, I am most conscious of her unflinching realism. She teaches us that we should love the world unconditionally, and find the reality and presence of God through all external things *without exception,* 'as clearly as our hand feels the substance of paper through the pen-holder and the nib'[15]. The world is as it is – we are not to wish for it to be otherwise as a material creation – and we must remain attentive to the possibil-ity of the transforming powers of suffering.

Weil is close to the spirit of the New Testament here in her recognition of the love of God in adversity. In a way that she could not have anticipated, but may have been prepared for through earlier experiences of pain, she was opened to a mysterious miracle of grace that turned her darkness to light. At the end of a year in which there had been many painful episodes, she had taken to reciting the poem 'Love', fixing her entire attention on the words:

Love bade me welcome: yet my soul drew back,
Guiltie of dust and sinne.
But quick-ey'd Love, observing me grow slack
From my first entrance in,
Drew nearer to me, sweetly questioning,
If I lack'd any thing.

A guest, I answered, worthy to be here:
Love said, You shall be he.
I the unkinde, ungratefull? Ah my deare,
I cannot look on thee.
Love took my hand, and smiling did reply,
Who made the eyes but I?

Truth Lord, but I have marr'd them: let my shame
Go where it doth deserve.
And know you not, sayes Love, who bore the blame?
My deare, then I will serve.
You must sit down, sayes Love, and taste my meat:
So I did sit and eat.[16]

The poem became a prayer almost without her realising it and she had the feeling that Christ was present. 'A presence more personal, more certain and more real than that of a human being'[17], she wrote to one correspondent. She also knew that it was not an apparition. To another friend and confidant she wrote: 'Moreover in this sudden possession of me by Christ, neither my senses nor my imagination had any part; I only felt in the midst of my suffering the presence of love, like that which can be read in the smile on a beloved face'[18].

Several things interest me here. Weil was not consciously seeking this kind of experience. She had too much strength of character to take refuge in any comforting illusions, and her intellect had put her on guard against this kind of temptation or the dangerous power of suggestion. Her philosophy up to this point had taught her to wait in patience rather than to seek, and whatever certainty or knowledge amounted to, their verification and truthfulness were, for her, bound up with what could be objectively measured. The last sentence she wrote in a notebook found after her death read: 'The most important part of education – to teach the meaning of *to know* (in the scientific sense).'[19] To this approach must be added the fact that by her own admission she had never read the mystics or contemplated the possibility of there being such a thing as real contact between a human being and God. If she was enthralled by the liturgy of the Church, and had for some time held aspects of Christianity in the highest regard, she was not a believer in the conventional sense of that term. Nothing had prepared her therefore in any obvious way for such an astonishing event. Now she had to contend with a transcendent God above and beyond the confines of rationality or science – the God of Abraham, Isaac and Jacob – and a Christ who had taken possession of her. Untutored and unpractised in prayer, and equating religion with morality and right action, she came to know Christ's presence and mercy in affliction. Even when the world assailed her, and contrary to much of her earlier philosophical understanding, she found it possible to affirm a deep and lasting experience of a loving God. We may be acutely aware of pain in our lives yet, for Weil, no less real are the moments of assurance when, by an act of divine grace, crucifixion and resurrection constitute one continuing process. In such instances suffering manifests a redemptive, even revelatory power that is consistent with the insight of the New Testament concerning One who learned obedience and was perfected 'through what he suffered' (Heb. 5:8).

After many griefs and disappointments, and the undoubted anguish she felt at the pains of others, Weil was able to live and write and continue her struggle. And there were consolations. She loved to smell the dew and rain, to delight in the constellation of the stars, the sound of silence and the purity of water. A little more than a year before her death, her photograph taken in New York reveals a gentleness, even serenity. Coming to London, she was able to speak tenderly of 'this city with its wounds'[20]. Even the room in which she would die became beautiful to her with its outlook of meadows and trees. Seven people attended her funeral on 30 August 1943. A priest had been asked to officiate but he never arrived. Someone said prayers and a bouquet tied with the colours of France was thrown into the grave. With hindsight, the scene can be viewed with pity, reverence, respect and gratitude. Prayers for a soul convicted of the truth that where there was a need there was an obligation. A *Tricolore*, to symbolise her love of nation and countrymen and the duty of resistance. And flowers, to testify that when afflicted she did indeed bud again, and in the hardest weather found an unexpected harbour in the real presence of Christ.

Notes

[1]   Quoted in Dorothee Soelle, *The Silent Cry* (Augsburg Fortress, 2001), p. 139.

[2]   Lucy Winkett, *Our Sound is Our Wound: Contemplative Listening to a Noisy World* (Continuum, 2010), p. 6.

[3]   The English writer George Eliot noted the following in her diary after reading Proust: 'Take up Proust and put him down. This is the worst time of all. It makes me suicidal. Nothing seems left to do. All seems insipid and worthless.' Eliot in fact went on to write *Middlemarch*, possibly the greatest English novel of the nineteenth century, which suggests that she came to terms with Proust's achievement by marking out her own distinctive terrain as a great author of unique sensibility and insight.

[4]   'Awake my soul and with the sun', *Hymns Ancient and Modern Revised* (William Clowes & Sons Ltd, 1922), No. 3, p. 2.

[5]   Further examples are provided by Alain de Botton in his accessible and wryly amusing *How Proust can Change your Life* (Picador, 1997), pp. 80–90.

[6]   See *Church Times,* 12 February 2010, p. 21.

[7]   Following his support of Captain Dreyfus, the Jewish army officer who was wrongly accused of betraying French records to the Germans, Proust lost some of his aristocratic friends and other influential people in high places.

[8]   de Botton, *How Proust,* p. 6.

[9]   In this respect Proust's insights may be usefully compared to the latest encyclical letter of Pope Benedict XVI in which he draws upon the teaching of his predecessor Paul VI. Benedict notes that in the pursuit of the development of the human person, there is a need for 'the deep thought and reflection of wise men in search of a new humanism which will enable modern man to find himself anew'. In relation to obstacles and forms of conditioning that impede our progress, he remains certain that none of us can relinquish the duty we have to exercise the responsible freedom that 'gives human life its true meaning'. See *Caritas in Veritate: Charity in Truth* (Veritas Publications, 2009), p. 20.19; p. 18.17; p. 20.18.

[10] Pseudonym of the well-known French philosopher and essayist, Emile Auguste Chartier (1868–1951).

[11] Simone Petrement, *Simone Weil* (Mowbrays, 1976), p. 471. Elsewhere she writes of the importance of preserving her freedom of thought: 'I do not recognise any right on the part of the Church to limit the workings of the intellect or the illuminations achieved by love in the domain of thought.' Petrement, *Simone Weil*, p. 523.

[12] Some of her essays and letters are published in Simone Weil, *Waiting on God: The Essence of her Thought* (Collins Fontana, 1973).

[13] Petrement, *Simone Weil*, p. 245.

[14] Petrement, *Simone Weil*, p. 516.

[15] Weil, *Waiting on God,* p. 14.

[16] George Herbert, 'Love', C. Ricks (ed.), *The Oxford Book of English Verse* (Oxford, 1999), p. 193.

[17] Petrement, *Simone Weil*, p. 340.

[18] Petrement, *Simone Weil*, p. 340.

[19] Weil, *Waiting on God,* p. 10.

[20] Petrement, *Simone Weil*, p. 512

CHAPTER 5

Remembrance of Things Past

A change of scenery is called for now — a movement away from the long shadow of the cross and a shift in location from Paris to a small town in Germany. From there, close on two centuries ago, we have an account of a young woman who could neither read nor write and was thought by priests to be a victim of demon possession because she was heard talking Latin, Greek and Hebrew when seized with a fever. Her ravings were written down and were found to consist of intelligible sentences with some connection to each other. A few of the Hebrew sayings were traced to the Bible, but most seemed to be in a Rabbinical dialect. Onlookers were baffled: the girl plainly had a fever and tricks were out of the question. The mystery was finally solved by a doctor, who, on tracing her history, found that at the age of nine she had been given a home by an old Protestant pastor, who was an accomplished Hebrew scholar. She remained in his care until his death. Further investigation by the physician revealed that it was the custom of the old man for many years to walk up and down a passage of his house reading aloud from his books. The passage was close to the kitchen. On examining the books after his death they were found to contain the writings of early Greek and Latin theologians accompanied by a collection of Rabbinical writings. In these works so many of the passages recorded at the young woman's bedside were identified that there could no longer be any reasonable doubt regarding their source.[1] After years of oblivion, and following the onset of a serious illness, deep experiences of her past came to life again with mysterious precision.

As I muse on this story, I think of one of my regular home communicants whom I first met more than ten years ago as she nursed her sick husband with great devotion. She is now in her late eighties and has serious dementia. As we sit quietly in her room and I remind her of who I am and why I have come, I dispense with books and service leaflets and rely on a recurring miracle. She remembers the prayers that we say together. The opening prayer to the God who knows our secret desires, the Confession, the Our Father and the closing prayer of Thanksgiving – all of these she recites by heart. So much of her past has slipped away from her, and, a few minutes after I have left, she will not remember my visit. But in these prayerful moments a single sentence brings her pleasure – 'Come unto me all ye that labour and are heavy laden and I will give you rest' – and she has the sense of being caught up in the great sea of faith that represents centuries of Christian tradition. Words repeated over and over again retain their ancient power, and memory weds her to the self she once was and the Christ in whom she has always found comfort.

Memory is one of the saving truths of our lives and is therefore a precious and redemptive faculty. It is not quite the same thing as consciousness but the two are intricately related. To remember is to have, as we have just noted, two selves, one in the memory and one thinking about the memory. In order to make any sense of our miraculous powers of recollecting and forgetting, we need pictures. Plato thought of the mind as a soft wax surface on which an image can be impressed, or as a gemstone in which it can be engraved or scratched. St Augustine famously thought of his memory as fields and spacious palaces where 'the treasures of innumerable forms be hoarded up'[2]. Thoughts, people and scenes lay within their boundaries and walls, often presenting themselves to him in an instant and sometimes sauntering into his mind as innocently as if they had never been summoned. Memory remained for Augustine a great and mysterious force that linked his nature to his past and represented the lodging of the Lord God ever since he had first learnt of 'him who hath made me and my nature'[3].

Augustine wrote extensively on a wide range of subjects. Gifted with explicit memory and a lively curiosity, recollections of his youth and childhood remained at the edge of his consciousness, ready to be called up and integrated into the emerging moments of his present. Other writers have possessed the same gift, and it is not surprising to learn that memory, or Mnemosyne, was, according to the Greeks, the mother of the Muses. Virginia Woolf was able to reach and record a state where she seemed to be watching things happen in her past as if she were there. Her memories of childhood days in St Ives became a form of rapture: the sound of waves breaking on the beach, the stir of going up to bed, the caw of the rooks in the early morning and the apples of red and gold in gardens that gave off a murmur of bees, made her years later 'feel warm; as if everything were ripe; humming; sunny'[4]. All these sound and colour memories had the power to stop her in her tracks and bless her with an ecstasy she could barely believe. What she was hearing, seeing, even smelling[5], with every startled breath she drew was a place forever associated with 'home'. If we are fortunate, many of us can draw on similar memories and experiences that, more poignantly, remind us of the past to which we long to return but cannot. D. H. Lawrence captures this ache in his poem 'Piano':

> Softly, in the dusk, a woman is singing to me;
> Taking me back down the vista of years, till I see
> A child sitting under the piano, in the boom of the tingling strings
> And pressing the small, poised feet of a mother who smiles as she sings.
>
> In spite of myself, the insidious mastery of song
> Betrays me back, till the heart of me weeps to belong
> To the old Sunday evenings at home, with winter outside
> And hymns in the cosy parlour, the tinkling piano our guide.
>
> So now it is vain for the singer to burst into clamour
> With the great black piano appassionato. The glamour
> Of childish days is upon me, my manhood is cast
> Down in the flood of remembrance, I weep like a child for the past.[6]

In these verses Lawrence recalls and elaborates a moment of lost time that is now imbued with the deepest feeling. What was once a routine occasion that made up the reliable fabric of family life is now a landmark that speaks of loss, the need for consolation and the continuous sense of his personal identity. As readers, we can look on this Sunday evening scene and perhaps recognise something of our own early years through its elegiac filter. But only Lawrence can feel it 'on the pulse', with an insistent homesickness that accompanies his remembering and a 'flashbulb' awareness that, despite all the wrecks and decays of time, the child under the piano and the poet recalling the scene are one and the same. So much has changed in the long and arduous interim: every cell of his body has been replaced; the texture and colour of his hair is different; his muscular strength is not as it was and the small patch of skin on the back of his hand tells its own story of instability and flux. Yet the memory he runs and reruns in his head corroborates his sense of self, whose name and DNA are shared with the child and make him 'I' or 'me' – those indispensable and incredible words that persevere through time as an abiding trace or pattern, giving shape and meaning[7] to the unrelated succession of days and a trusted 'point of convergence from which everything is viewed, measured and recounted'[8].

This assumed sense of personal identity is a blessing that is not always counted until we recognise its provenance. Our world of little everyday rituals, from getting up in the morning to going to bed at night, and the vaster world of the Earth moving round the Sun at thirty kilometres per second, is gifted to us by the fixed idea that we have of ourselves as persons blessed with a viewpoint that enables us to make some sense of the objective universe, and convinces us that even if we gaze in the mirror and see a strange face looking back, our sense of self, though shaken, would still persist. We abide through change as an 'I' or 'me' because our minds are supported by the cornerstone of memory, that safe stronghold of our past and the window through which we have access to the unceasing traffic of things out there, from frozen pizza to the great and dependable silence of the night sky.

In yet another way, memory is the midwife of our moral imagination and the potential source of our compassion and penitence as we seek to negotiate a proper sense of our past. It is for this reason that Augustine also defines memory as 'spirit'. In recollection, he finds not only the intimations of an everlasting love that he desires and will not let him go, but also the self he was that said or did particular and painful things at specific times. In the 'vast cloisters' of his memory he is led both to God and the awareness of his own moral incompleteness – the back catalogue of unkindnesses or cruelties that invariably diminish all human lives. The crucial issue here is what we do with the instances where we got it wrong, even hopelessly wrong. We can resort to denial and refuse to face the mess we made. We can claim for ourselves the status of victim – that our lapses owed everything to the prior hurts and rejections we experienced at the hands of others. Or we can own up and, in a spirit of resolve and contrition, use the recollections of past failures to generate a 'catholicity of sympathy ... that reaches out to the incompleteness of others'[9]. Augustine is venerated chiefly as a great sinner who became a great saint, and a strong adversary of heretics and enemies of the Church. But we should also recall that he was a diligent and conscientious pastor overseeing clergy and congregations where mediocrity and waywardness were commonplace. The record indicates that he was slow to condemn and forgiving of those who had fallen short or lost their way.[10] He kept the mercy of the Lord in mind (a mercy that he knew from personal experience to be real) and in the remembrance of his own transgressions he sought the forgiveness of others and tried to love them as brothers in Christ.[11]

If we bear a responsibility for the misery we have strewn as individuals along the way, and look to memory to redeem it by confronting us with the sorry facts in order that we might learn from them, the moral duty of remembrance also taxes our collective imagination. As nations, we have good cause to acknowledge the barbarism and madness unleashed in the name of wars and ideologies or the quest for power, and it is memory which ensures that history grants us no armistice or exemption from the inhuman. The grand set pieces of Remembrance Sunday, with their calibrated and poignant moments, pass a solemn but all too brief warning down the years as they commemorate the dead of former conflicts. For a few minutes the world is stilled until the bugle is sounded and the yield of a country coming together is soon spent. But, with attention and persistence, memory can do more than this. It can evoke in the imagination of communities – assemblies of decency, desire, resistance and faith – a renewed commitment to hope, to reconfigure mourning in the sense of lamentation, into the promise of daybreak or a new dawn. Monuments to the fallen stand everywhere, but it is only when we stop and look that something of significance happens. A familiar scene is described by the writer and critic George Steiner:

> On our way to and from Cambridge so many of us pass,
> perhaps unheeding, in front of the memorial in Liverpool

Street station to the railway workers who fell in the First World War. Their names fill columns on a high wall. When I pass by, I pick a name at random and attempt a simple thought-experiment. I try to picture the man named, to envision him during the long, idyllic summer of 1914 or in the murderous stench of the trenches. I try to evoke the old age he will not have known and, in the case of those who fell young, to sense the weight of absence, the tear in the fabric of natural life caused by the fact that this man will have fathered no children, known no grandchildren, that by this man's early death we remain deprived.[12]

Here memory moves from the Somme, and a life forfeited for no great cause, to a future burdened by a felt absence and the failure of promise struck down. Steiner goes on, however, to urge his listeners to hope:

> The congregation of memory of which we are a part, the covenant of scrupulous imagining and of silence in which we are joined, extend far beyond the compass of any religious service or denomination. They should, however imperfectly, mesh all who dwell in history. They should create a bond between all who know that the trusteeship of life entails not only the task of remembrance but that of conveyance, that the earth is ours only if we labour to hand it on to coming generations a little saner, a mite cleaner than we found it.[13]

A congregation of memory is a deeply affecting image. The idea that silence, prayer and painstaking recollection can combine to embrace the waste of war, the duty to safeguard the precious remnants of Eden and 'discharge in some part at least, our debt to the wonder and fragility of being'[14], is to honour as pressing and precious that which could yet be. In the restraint and beauty of a Cambridge University chapel, a secular Jew of great intellectual distinction, whose mind is never far from the atrocities of the Nazi Holocaust, urges his listeners to make a pact with their memory for the sake of the future and to honour, *in memoriam,* 'the maimed and the mentally and spiritually scarred for whom every day is remembrance day'[15]. He reminds them that this duty is universal in its scope and is not confined to households of faith alone.

This last comment makes me wonder if Steiner might have read the obituary of Tsutomu Yamaguchi, a Buddhist and a double nuclear survivor of the atomic bombs that fell on Hiroshima and Nagasaki, who died recently, aged 93. He was two miles from the epicentre of the first blast on 6 August 1945. The upper half of his body and half of his face were badly burned, his hair disappeared and his eardrums were ruptured. He tried to get back to the devastated city but the river bridges were down. One river was full of carbonised naked bodies of men, women and children, floating face-down like blocks of wood. Clambering on to these 'human rafts', he got to the other side. When he reached Nagasaki, barely pausing to have his wounds tended, the same ominous white magnesium light blazed again. His bandages were blown off and he spent the following weeks in a shelter close to death. He survived, but could not forget the mute, naked, limping children on the streets or the floating bodies in the river. Eventually he returned to work and much later in life wrote a book of poems called *The Human Raft*. He began to feel that his destiny was to remind a new generation of the horrors of nuclear weapons and the dark ambivalences of human nature.[16] Aged 90, on his first trip abroad, he read aloud in front of a committee of the United Nations in New York:

> If there exists a God who protects
> nuclear-free eternal peace
> the blue earth won't perish.[17]

In great old age he found comfort in painting and in simple acts of kindness. Most consoling of all was the image of his life as a baton, passed on every time a college student, politician or American President heard or read his testimony. From the charnel house of his memory he rescued a testimony to share with others in the belief that all these batons might form, together, another human raft. I have a picture before me that shows Yamaguchi sitting silently and peacefully in his garden, hands clasped together on the top of his walking stick. The sunlight bathes his forehead and his stillness evokes the knowing image of the Buddha who has no need to speak. In repose, Yamaguchi is perhaps recalling all the lost and voiceless who perished, including his own son Katsutoshi who died at 59, killed by the radiation he had received as a baby. The old man's gaze, steady and unperturbed, looks beyond the shadows of the garden to the distant hills and, beyond those, to a future for humanity free from violence.

Instinctively, I want to pause here – partly out of respect for the shared vision of Steiner and Yamaguchi, but also to revisit the claims advanced in this chapter. Memory is gift. In its ample fields the past is held for us along with our enduring identity that holds a tremulous world together. Memory is our conscience and guide: individually and collectively it holds up to us an earth that we have scorched with our fallibilities in the hope that we can and must do better. Memory engenders the sympathy which acknowledges that we all come from a common clay and should therefore forgive. Following Augustine, it is also the movement of the mind that leads us Godward in the direction of an everlasting love that redeems the fragmented, wayward and assertive selves that we are. In one of Charles Wesley's hymns, the Holy Spirit is designated 'Remembrancer Divine' – 'the one who makes the past of Jesus present to us now'[18]. In the breaking of bread and the abiding memory of a divine command 'to do this', first spoken by a young Jew in the presence of his friends in an Upper Room on the night before he died, generations of faithful souls for a hundred thousand Sundays and more have continued to find a means of grace that opens up the road to God. And even when much has been taken away through age or frailty, pure gold remains: the prayers we learn from others; the texts that illuminate our darkness; the comfortable words that soften even the solitude of dementia and join a lonely woman's heart to the hearts of others in pilgrimage, as they too seek the gates of Zion.[19]

If we pay attention to all of this – the command obeyed century after century[20] and the events recalled and made present in the Eucharist that speak of a death like no other, a stone rolled away and incredulous disciples running at the break of day to an empty tomb – we shall be struck by the enduring power of the Christian gospel and the pivotal place of memory at its centre. The past is never really past at the altar of God, for there it is folded into the present to become the means of redemption and reconciliation in a turbulent world. For this story 'so divine', and for the grace of remembrance, there is only thanks and still more thanks.

Notes

1   Cited in *Biographia Literaria,* 1847, edn 1. 117.
2   St Augustine, *Confessions,* Book X (Penguin Classics, 1961).
3   Augustine, *Confessions,* Book X.
4   Virginia Woolf, *Moments of Being* (Hogarth Press, 1985 edition).
5   In 2004 the Nobel Prize for Physiology was given to two American scientists, Richard Axel and Linda Buck, for a remarkable paper on the connection between the nose and the brain. They demonstrated that the nose has nearly a thousand separate 'receptors' (ten times more than a fish but forty times less than a dog). They form unique clusters or 'olfactory patterns' which are capable of 'holding memories of approximately 10,000 different odours' (Nobel Prize press release, 4 October 2004).
6   Cited in A. S. Byatt and H. H. Wood (eds.), *Memory: An Anthology* (Chatto and Windus, 2008), p. 131. Lawrence was frequently ill as a child and developed a deep and passionate bond with his mother. Poor health dogged his short life but he always remained grateful to his mother for her love and encouragement.
7   'Memory performs the impossible for man by the strength of his divine arms; holds together past and present, beholding both, existing in both, abides in the flowing and gives continuity and dignity to human life. It holds us to our family, to our friends. Hereby a home is possible; hereby only a new fact has value.' Part of lecture given by Ralph Waldo Emerson on 12 November 1879. Cited by David Shank, *The Forgetting* (Flamingo Press, 2003).
8   Michael Frayn, *The Human Touch: Our Part in the Creation of a Universe* (Faber & Faber, 2006), p. 401.
9   Rowan Williams, *Open to Judgement: Sermons and Addresses* (Darton, Longman and Todd, 1994), p. 210.
10 Augustine did not flinch from administering rebukes when they were justified but it caused him much inward pain. As a bishop he was depressed by human weakness but in his writings he tried to provide his people with the nourishment that was also necessary for his own fragile nature. At a personal level, his own experience did not make him intolerant but compassionate and he was quick to urge parishioners to suspend judgement in situations where they did not know the secrets of others' souls. See Garry Wills, *St Augustine* (Weidenfeld & Nicholson, 1999), p. 135, and Peter Brown, *Augustine of Hippo: A Biography* (Faber & Faber, 1969), p. 278.
11 *Confessions,* p. 247. It is significant that in the long struggle against the Donatists who believed that they alone represented the true Church,

Augustine found violence abhorrent and urged his fellow Catholics not to be uncharitable even when their buildings and clergy came under attack. See Henry Chadwick, *Augustine* (Oxford University Press, 1986), pp. 77–79.

[12] The opening of an address given at King's College chapel, Cambridge, on Remembrance Sunday 1989 and later published in the Cambridge Review.

[13] George Steiner, Remembrance Sunday address. For a philosophical exploration of the duty of remembrance see Avishai Margalit, *The Ethics of Memory* (Harvard Press, 2003).

[14] Steiner Address.

[15] Steiner Address.

[16] In another context the Polish philosopher, Leszek Kolakowski coined the aphorism: 'We learn history not in order to know how to behave or how to succeed, but to know who we are.' See *The Economist*, 14 August 2009.

[17] Cited in the obituary in *The Economist*, 16 January 2010. The Japanese government officially designated Yamaguchi the only *nijyuu hibakusha*, or twice-victim of the atom bomb (though there had been more than 100 others).

[18] Rowan Williams, *Open to Judgement*, p. 241.

[19] This image is captured perfectly in the closing verses of Psalm 48:

> Walk about Zion, go all around it, count its towers,
> consider well its ramparts;
> go through its citadels,
> that you may tell the next generation that this is God,
> our God for ever and ever
> He will be our guide for ever.

(vv. 12–14)

[20] See Gregory Dix, *The Shape of the Liturgy* (A & C Black, 1945), pp. 744–745 for a moving account of how the command 'to do this' has been honoured in so many different contexts throughout Christian history.

◦⟨⟩◦

CHAPTER 6

The Language of Beauty

In keeping with my closing thoughts in the last chapter, it seems right to register my personal gratitude for the texts, prayers and stories that have become a permanent feature of my mind. They represent the fixtures, a sort of 'second canon' of words and images that I have committed to memory and, more importantly, have stayed there! For me they carry authority and continue to shape the person I am and still hope to become. Earlier this morning, working in my study and in need of inspiration, I listened to Johann Sebastian Bach's *Cello Suites*. I have loved his music for most of my adult life and have never forgotten an article written many years ago by the journalist Katherine Whitehorn. In it, she revealed how Bach always managed to raise her spirits: just one movement of any of the Brandenburg Concertos could ease dark thoughts. Her experience encouraged me to discover the solace of these and other extraordinary masterworks associated with Bach that have come to represent a musical Everest in the classical repertoire. In this respect, I understand rather better now than I could have possibly done then, the decision of the Italian cellist Mario Brunello in 2007 to climb to the summit of Mount Fuji, almost 3,750 metres above sea level, in order to play selections from the *Cello Suites*. Explaining the reasons behind the climb and his choice of music, he declared that 'Bach's music comes closest to the absolute and to perfection'[1]. It's an image worth committing to memory, and in its daring and determination represents a brave and imaginative testament to the lure of beauty.

Confronted with beauty, we face a paradox: on the one hand its value is self-evident and its promise intoxicating – even mountains are climbed in its honour. On the other hand, it is also difficult – note the way in which philosophers over time have required an ocean of ink to fathom beauty's depths, only to discover its mystery eluding them.[2] Beauty also comes down to the matter of perception and 'the eye of the beholder': as the poet Blake observed, to one person a tree is 'just a green thing', and to another a thing of beauty. Blake knew from his own experience as an artist that public taste and private responses are often shallow, or simply skewed, and bear little or no relation to the object in view. To the discerning eye, his late woodcut engravings afforded 'complete and unreserved delight'[3] and a glimpse of heaven enjoyed by saints and sages. More fickle viewers, however, in the restless search for novelty, found his work obscure or quaint and his humour bitter. Like the later paintings of Turner, the late string quartets of Beethoven and the final piano sonatas of Schubert (all from the same period of the 1820s), the beauty of Blake's imagination was neither fully understood nor properly appreciated at the time. It became the task and privilege of later generations to see and hear sublime things anew.

Once we recognise the pitfalls and problems surrounding beauty, we can still testify to its power. In its restraint and elusiveness, and without ever having to explain itself, beauty delights, beguiles, comforts, inspires and – a key word in this chapter – *transports* us to what the eminent literary critic Harold Bloom calls 'the ecstasy of the privileged moment'. Beauty is about rapture, transformation and joy. In her lovely and provocative book *Art Objects*[4], the writer Jeanette Winterson describes a heart-stopping moment in Amsterdam one snowy Christmas as she passed a small gallery and was overwhelmed by a painting in the window. After recovering in a nearby bookshop, in the relative calm of the familiar, she changed her travel plans and spent afternoons in galleries and evenings 'reading, reading, reading' in order to find a guide who could help her negotiate this new and foreign country of paintings. Back home, in the shelter of second-hand bookshops, she found a mentor and also discovered within herself a growing conviction that great art constitutes a certain kind of fixed point in a floating world and opens up the heart to beauty.

Art in all its forms invites, even commands, us to be still and fills our minds with unexpected light. In this respect, words in particular have proved irresistible for Winterson and myself. The spell they cast remains mysterious (as it should). If it has something to do with the innate loveliness of certain words and phrases, and the seemliness and order achieved through good syntax, it is also bound up with their energy that invites us to live more deeply and to rediscover the intensity of the material world.

Reading Rupert Brooke's poem 'The Great Lover' for the first time in early adolescence, I related to his evocation of 'wet roofs beneath the lamplight … the good smell of old clothes and the rough male kiss of blankets'. The images pleased me and I recognised them immediately in much the same way that tulips and roses belong in the predictable category of sunrises, a full moon, kingfishers and butterflies, rainbows and burning leaves and most small children. But one phrase in the poem left me reeling – 'the benison of hot water'. I lacked a local bookstore to stagger into for the purpose of recovery but the ecstasy was real and I was happy to remain dazed. It was the word 'benison' in particular that would not go away. Around and around it turned in my mind before finally settling there forever. What I could not understand at the time (and in a sense it didn't really matter, such was the power of the moment) was that it was the beauty of the word that had changed me. All I knew was that I had been gifted by a solitary word whose meaning was unknown to me. Only later would I discover that the correlates of 'benison' include benediction and blessing.

Because they are beautiful, language, poetry and paintings, along with music, have the power to heal and transform. Poetry can cleanse our wounds and words have the power to conserve our sanity and strength. After a troubled but strangely rewarding upbringing by an adoptive fundamentalist Christian mother and a father who seemed largely absent, Winterson left a home where the assiduous reading of the Bible was mandatory, in order to support herself and continue her education. She staved off loneliness and fear by reciting the long Bible passages and poetry that she had memo-rised as a child. In the funeral parlour where she found work, she 'whispered Donne to the embalming fluids and Marvell to the corpses'[5]. Later, she discovered that Tennyson's 'Lady of Shalott' had a calming effect on the mentally disturbed, among whose number she included herself at the time. She had grown up in the belief that the Word was God. Having relinquished the evangelical certainties of childhood, she continued to think of language as something holy and redemptive. It raised her up, served as her rod and staff, her resting place and shield and a gateway to the sublime. We are not surprised to find her quoting Blake:

> How do you know but every
> bird that cuts the airy way
> Is an immense world of delight
> closed by your senses five?[6]

In 1978 she packed her few possessions into the back of a Morris Minor van and drove to Oxford to read English. Initially she found it hard to believe that everyone was expected to read widely and think for themselves in an atmosphere where learning was an end in itself. Quite soon she also discovered that her knowledge of the Bible gave her a huge advantage over other students. She knew about the burning bush, the still small voice and the valley of the shadow in a way that was not merely theoretical. The images and sounds of scripture had already possessed her and she grasped more quickly than others the extent to which a holy book had enlivened and sculpted the English language through the works of Milton, Bunyan, Wordsworth, D. H. Lawrence and Eliot. The beauty and religious ecstasy of the Bible, and poets such as George Herbert who embody its sensibilities, remain for her, a generation later, 'talismans of intensity' that feed and challenge her extraordinary imagination and creative word-play as a writer.

If we rewind at this point to Winterson's childhood in a town full of chimneys, cobbled roads, little shops and back-to-back houses with no gardens and outside toilets where spiders unhelpfully emerge from nearby coalsheds[7], we can see her mother at prayer in the front room. Her wish is to raise her child as a servant of God in the hope that she will eventually become a missionary. Mother has a preference for the Old Testament, and is not much given to 'gentle Jesus, meek and mild'. She tunes in to radio evangelists and is an active member of the Society for the Lost. She is energetic, driven, organised and keen to change the world. Above most things scriptural, she favours the Book of Deuteronomy, especially its laws, statutes and ordinances that permeate Chapters 12 to 26. She teaches her daughter to read from it. The child complies, but her attention (sometimes openly, more often furtively) shifts elsewhere

in the text. She is exposed to the God of the Israelites who leads
them out of slavery in a 'pillar of cloud by day and a pillar of fire by
night' (Exod. 13:21). She sees the tower of Babel reaching into
heaven (Gen. 11:4) and its builders scattered abroad and their
language confused. She turns the pages to another city, this time to
the Book of Revelation, and encounters the New Jerusalem with its
great high wall built of jasper, its street 'pure gold, transparent as
glass' (21:21), its God – the ineffable Face that is its light and lamp –
and the woman crowned with stars (12:1). The names of the Old
Testament books are remembered, and one day they will serve as the
chapter titles of Winterson's first highly-acclaimed novel, written at
the age of 24.[8] But it is the language and what it discloses to her that
will be reconstructed and then translated on to a different canvas
with the aim of seeing into the life of things.[9] In her fiction,
Winterson presents us with new geographies and worlds that are
familiar, but also strange and steeped in unimagined possibilities. For
her, the contemporary city sings in praise of the present moment and
its claim on our attention and response. As she sets down the beauty
before her eyes, Winterson challenges us to see the city in a transfigured light – a light that for her has its genesis in childhood memories,
in a vision that brings the New Testament to a close and a book in
which she has found meanings behind meanings:[10]

> Up higher, far away, the red digital flash of date and time:
> November 10 19:47 (Sun in Scorpio. City of New York).
> Blue sky light had turned black, red tracks of automobiles
> wound across the bridge, safety lights on brake reflectors, red
> on red.
> The universe hangs here, in this narrow strait, infinity and
> compression caught in the hour. Space and time cannot be
> separated. History and futurity are now. What you remember.
> What you invent. The universe curving in your gut. Put out
> your hand. Kiss me. The city is a scintilla, light to light, quartz
> and neon of the Brooklyn bridge and the incandescence of the
> stars.
> They were letting off fireworks down at the waterfront, the sky
> exploding in grenades of colour. Whatever it is that pulls the
> pin, that hurls you past the boundaries of your own life into a
> brief and total beauty, even for a moment, it is enough.[11]

I am guessing here but my strong hunch is that her mother would struggle to see any scriptural resonances in the above passage. In her Bible there are chiefly strenuous commands, mortal threats, and the perpetual fight against the Evil One. 'Thou shall not' tends to overshadow moments of being. But in a curious way I warm to her. She is not without qualities. There is something endearing in the image of a mother sitting down with her daughter on the beach at Blackpool to draw the animals recorded in the book of Deuteronomy. She brings pelicans, rock badgers, sloths and bats, winged insects and birds of the air vividly to life, and they assume a greater prominence in the child's mind than the horses, bunnies and little ducks that other children love and talk about.[12] And this is a feisty woman. She knows, *really* knows (if only partially), the scriptures that sustain her. When a spotty youth starts banging on the walls of her home to stop the loud hymn singing, she confronts him fearlessly and directly with words from Deuteronomy: 'The Lord will smite you with the boils of Egypt and with the ulcers and scurvy and the itch of which you cannot be cured'. With the moaning of the heathen stilled, she returns inside having slammed the backdoor. 'Now then,' she smiles, 'who's for a bit of dinner?'[13]

We should smile too at this scene, but it's not unproblematic. A home frequently berated by neighbours because of rousing choruses that threaten to wake the dead is, we must concede, an unlikely lodging place for the sublime. Likewise, even her smiling invitation to dinner might cause us to hesitate. A tablecloth with the daunting words 'DEEDS OF THE OLD TESTAMENT' embroidered on it does not suggest that we are about to sit down in order to contemplate the generosity of God in the gracious sharing of food and hospitality. A religion predicated on deeds alone has no time for timeless moments. Similarly, moral earnestness (however genuine or endearing) can easily blind us to the spirit of beauty that breathes through the words of scripture. God places man in the Garden of Eden to do more than cultivate it and keep his commandments. St Paul, for all his abstemiousness, recognises this and points us to all things lovely and true that transport us to the realm of absolute beauty (Phil. 4:8) that is the throne of God (Rev. 20:11). Elsewhere, like the proverbial thread of gold, instance after instance in the biblical record shows individuals caught up and taken beyond themselves in contemplation and awe.

Paul bows his knees before the Father; Thomas, no longer doubting the reality of the risen Christ, can only utter 'My Lord and my God'; when Elizabeth is greeted by Mary, she is filled with the Spirit and her unborn child John leaps in her womb for joy; on the road to Emmaus, two forlorn disciples suddenly feel their hearts burn as the Christ they initially fail to recognise opens up the scriptures for them. A moment of illumination renders transparent the meaning of 'Moses and all the prophets' (Luke 24:27) and, later at table, they behold the fair beauty of the Lord in the blessing, breaking and sharing of bread (Luke 24:30). High on a mountain top, Peter, James and John are overcome as the face of Jesus shines like the sun when he is transfigured before them (Matt. 17:2); on another road, between Galilee and Jerusalem, a man who has walked in darkness all his life is touched by Jesus and, having washed in the pool of Siloam, receives his sight. In dazed gratitude he can only affirm to the questioning crowd: 'One thing I do know, that though I was blind, now I see' (John 9:25). It takes a long time for the disciples of Jesus to see. But, with his final words to them before his withdrawal into heaven, they return to Jerusalem with great joy, as men and women who have been blessed and therefore changed (Luke 24:50–53).

What is true of the New Testament extends to the Hebrew scriptures. Beyond the legalism of Deuteronomy we discover moments of longing and recognition – epiphanies that mark individuals for ever and set their feet in a new direction. Jacob is left alone and wrestles in the dark with a divine being until the dawn. In the struggle Jacob's hip is put out of joint, but finally he is blessed. He limps towards the sunrise the same man as he was before, yet also changed. He has a new name (Israel) and, in his own words, he has 'seen God face to face, and yet my life is preserved' (Gen. 32:30). The vision of God – the God who invests us with the desire for beauty – is also the solitary plea of the Psalmist: 'One thing I asked of the Lord, that I will seek after; to live in the house of the Lord all the days of my life, to behold the beauty of the Lord, and to inquire in his temple (Ps. 27:4). It is in the temple that the prophet Isaiah is blessed: conscious only of his unworthiness before the throne of

God, his lips are touched by the burning presence of an angel and, like Jacob, he now finds himself in a different landscape. He hears the call of God to go to his people and eagerly responds with the words that have sealed so many missionary endeavours since: 'Here am I; send me!' (Isa. 6:8). Beauty courses through such language and does not have to threaten or coerce in order to elicit our allegiance. Because it is of God, it is, in the end irresistible, as both the Psalmist and poet attest:

> I love all beauteous things,
> I seek and adore them;
> God hath no better praise,
> And man in hasty days
> Is honoured for them.[14]

It is possible that in my earlier remarks concerning Winterson's mother, and her sincere but limited approach to scriptures, I might have done her an injustice. Perhaps she had more than a passing acquaintance with the encounters I have just mentioned or others like them. In unguarded moments when the pressing voice of duty receded, maybe she found some texts attractive, even persuasive. Not quite persuasive enough, however. Drawing animals on the beach for an endlessly curious child and singing the rousing tunes of the *Redemption Hymnal* is about as close as she gets to the gateway of rapture. The language and images of the Bible seem not to soften her. Holy writ, by and large, is her strong tonic for the flagging spirit and the means whereby she remains 'fastened to the rock' in the difficult pursuit of perfection. Hymns ensure that she does not wobble:

> Yield not to temptation, for
> yielding is sin,
> Each victory will help you
> some other to win.

> Fight manfully onwards, Dark
> Passions subdue,
> Look ever to Jesus, He will
> carry you through.

Once again I'm forced to admire her resoluteness and the power of hymnody to uphold her as a missionary on the home front. Luminaries of her acquaintance, such as Pastor Spratt, embark on trips to Africa with the Glory Crusade. She stays local, listening to Johnny Cash as she prepares a new handout on baptism by total immersion, or thinking about the trifles and mound of cheese and onion sandwiches she has to prepare for the imminent visit of Pastor Finch from Stockport, who is to speak to the church on how easy it is to become demon possessed.[15] She is constantly absorbed and committed, but there is a void in her life. She deserves to be immersed in something more oceanic than a baptismal policy. The great omission is that she has been starved of the spell of the story. She uses her eyes to stop her from bumping into things but somehow they fail to capture the order and harmony so evident in the book of God – the awesome mystery of the beginning of creation, the living breath of the Lord forming life from the dust, the bestowal of the Sabbath rest and the poignant ache which touches everything under the sun (Eccles. 1). There is a great cosmic drama going on and the sacred scrolls convey this by setting down history, romance, poems, psalms, proverbs, love-songs, visions of the End and a gleaming city. In all their varied beauty they have the power to transform and transport, and to confer a blessing upon us. What they ask for in return is our reverence, the attitude that leads our hearts and hopes beyond the text and even the creation itself to the Creator, and the holiness and beauty that inform the humblest thing.[16]

Unfortunately our intrepid and dedicated local evangelist gets none of this. Beauty has passed her by because she sees the Bible as a single book that is best translated as a moral code. Despite the fact that many before and since have thought in such terms this still represents a sorry mistake, and for two reasons. First, as the biblical scholar James Barr has pointed out:

In biblical times, the books were separate individual scrolls. A 'Bible' was not a volume one could hold in the hand, but a cupboard or chest with pigeonholes, or a room or cave with a lot of individual scrolls. The boundary between what was scripture and what were other holy books was thus more difficult to indicate, and so was the order of the books and the organisation (if any) of the canon.[17]

We are not talking here about a collection of 'little books' (from the Greek *ta biblia*), or something comparable to the assembled works of Shakespeare. What is placed before us amounts to a window on people, events and teaching – an inspired and inspiring literature, illuminating our human situation and pointing us beyond that to a reality outside itself. Many voices from different times come together in its pages as the compelling Word of God. But the Bible was not a book to Jeremiah or St Paul or Jesus – a fact that most of us continue to overlook. When Jesus comes to the synagogue in Nazareth on the Sabbath day, he reads from the scroll. After expounding Isaiah, he rolls it up again and gives it back to the attendant (Luke 4:16–20). It is patently more than just words on paper, but it is a scroll and not a book.

As God's liberating word (and here we come to our second reason), scrolls do more than keep us on the narrow way. Too many readers of scripture have come to believe that the Bible has been written with an iron pen, and that God represents 'three angry letters in a book'. The problem with this view (even when we concede that evidence can be found to support it) is that it plays down or ignores the three pillars of scripture – creation, revelation and redemption. In placing so much emphasis on judgement and wrath, the tidings of comfort, mystery and joy that are 'far more precious than jewels' (Prov. 31:10) go unheeded. Once we grasp that the Bible has a more gracious purpose than that of finding us out in order to reprove, we can engage with it and trust the text to see where it will lead us. Captivated and enchanted by the sonorousness of its language and the beauty to which it testifies, we can, like Jacob, move towards the rising sun.

I hope that Jeanette Winterson might approve of the above image. Think of her as we close, leaving the family home where, we recall, the Word was God. She is uncertain of her destiny but, in a way that she cannot know just now, she has already been blessed. Her imagination has yielded to sacred words 'written with black fire on white fire and lying in the lap of God'[18]. One day, rather like the cellist who graced the opening page of this chapter, she too will scale mountains where she will cast her own spells in homage to beauty.

Notes

1. Eric Sibley, *The Cello Suites: In Search of a Baroque Masterpiece* (Harvill Secker, 2010), p. 6.
2. For an interesting and visually stunning account, see Umberto Eco (ed.), *On Beauty: A History of a Western Idea*, (Secker & Warburg, 2004).
3. Marilyn Butler, *Romantics, Rebels and Reactionaries: English Literature and its Background 1760–1830* (Oxford University Press, 1981), p. 53.
4. Jeanette Winterson, *Art Objects: Essays on Ecstasy and Effrontery* (Jonathan Cape, 1995).
5. Winterson, *Art Objects*, p. 156.
6. William Blake, *The Marriage of Heaven and Hell* (c.1790).
7. Jeanette Winterson, *Oranges are not the Only Fruit* (Vintage, 2001), p. 6.
8. Winterson, *Oranges*.
9. Alberto Manguel, 'The End of Reading' in *A Reader on Reading* (Yale University Press, 2010), pp. 288–291, provides an interesting account of 'creative hermeneutics' and the way in which the declared intentions of an author are invariably changed and extended by the experience, reason and imagination of the reader.
10. The Church Father Jerome (345–420) was led to remark that the book of Revelation contained as many mysteries as it contains words. The great theologian and philosopher Origen (185–254) exclaimed: 'Who can read the revelations granted to John without being amazed at the hidden depths of the ineffable mysteries, a depth apparent even to the person who does not understand what the text says?' (*On First Principles*, 4.2.4.).
11. Winterson, *Gut Symmetries*, cited in Denis Donoghue, *Speaking of Beauty* (Yale University Press, 2003), p. 185.
12. Winterson, *Oranges*, p. 41.
13. Winterson, *Oranges*, p. 53.
14. Robert Bridges, *I Love All Beauteous Things* (1876).
15. Winterson, *Oranges*, p. 11.
16. Augustine came to this insight and awareness late but reverence eventually became for him one meaning of *confessio* – 'the recognition of the God who unaccountably made everything to exist simply because He loved and is love'. See Robert J. O'Connell SJ, *Art and the Christian Intelligence in St Augustine* (Blackwell, 1978), p. 157.
17. James Barr, *Holy Scripture: Canon, Authority, Criticism* (Oxford, 1983).
18. Midrash on Psalms 90:3 in Louis Ginsberg, *The Legends of the Jews* (Philadelphia, 1913), p. 1.

-✠-

CHAPTER 7

In Praise of Laughter

By now you will not be surprised to learn that my personal lexicon of the beautiful and true would have to include writers and poets, artists and musicians. They bring lustre and meaning to my life, and, if heaven has no exalted stage for Bach, I may well seek admission to the other place! I am also hopeful that the best comedians will be seated at the top table at the great banquet of the blessed. They will be there doing what they love best, delighting the diverse assembly of holy fools, faithful souls and – surprise, surprise – the honest doubters and sceptics who never quite managed to swallow the Creeds but impressed the Lord by the integrity of their lives. Like the comedians, they gave much to others on earth and now find themselves recipients of an unexpected reward.

One of my most cherished memories of a Manchester childhood is walking home with my father from a matinee Christmas panto at the Ardwick Hippodrome. The early evening is cold and still, and the afterglow of the performance binds us together. I recall very little of the show but can still see Tommy Cooper emerging periodically, stage right, clutching a toy animal that grows larger with each appearance. Tommy, predictably, never speaks a word, but his fez, his crazed smile and animated face, and just the way he keeps pointing in bewilderment to the pet that initially snuggles in his arms and then grows so big that he can barely carry it leave the audience helpless. The laughter is long, innocent and life-giving, and seems all of a piece with the joy of the Season. Later, at my local church, where I sing in the choir, the carols tell of the angels making mirth at the birth of the Christ child. Their delight knows no bounds and the praise of the heavenly host resounds with laughter that such a marvellous thing should bless a broken world.

I am keen to write about laughter in this chapter, but not without hesitation. Time spent laughing is a foretaste of heaven and the gift to make others laugh is to unearth the possibilities of the sacred in our midst. Without humour, I doubt that my faith and ministry would have survived until now. Each new day continues to bring instances of the ridiculous and absurd that temper the tragedies and disappointments of what Augustine called our 'common mortal life'[1], along with those ordinary moments when keeping a straight face is almost heroic. I can only smile inwardly as I gently suggest to a surprised bride-to-be that the theme music to *Jaws* is perhaps not the best choice for the entrance music to her wedding, quite apart from the effect it might have on the concentration of the junior choristers. Similarly, a request from a motorcycling fraternity brings a slight twitch to the corner of my mouth. Scores of their number wished to assemble in church to pay their last farewells to a respected friend. They turned up on the appointed day and the pews were filled with bikers whose jackets uniformly bore the fierce inscription 'Satan's Slaves'. They proved a model congregation and, as ever, I was left wondering about the fuzzy line that ostensibly separates the righteous from the lost.

My reservations about laughter, particularly as it touches the religious life, are fourfold. Writing or reading about humour – how it works and why – often results in seriously unfunny prose. It's as if the attempt to explain the comic and daft contrives to rob them of their inner mystery, energy and joy. The proper stance here is to let humour be and simply marvel at its power to transform and heal. In his semi-autobiographical novel, *The Stark Munro Letters*[2], Arthur Conan Doyle relishes the stars in the sky precisely because he doesn't understand them: 'I am proud to say that I don't know the name of one of them. The glamour and romance would pass away from them if they were all classified and ticketed in one's brain.' A willed ignorance is perhaps not also a bad thing in relation to the cosmos that is laughter.

The fact that humour is so vast in its scope, origins and scale, raises two related difficulties. Most of us love a good laugh, and laughter makes and keeps us human. Historically, most authors depict Man as the only creature who was created able to laugh.[3] Chimpanzees go through the motions but try telling them a joke about a man who goes into a bar and they will not be deflected from devouring their bananas. A regrettable problem with human beings is that sometimes they invite us to laugh at the wrong things. Some weeks ago, I was invited to say a few words at the beginning of a charity dinner. The room was packed with football enthusiasts, all in a lively mood and ready to pay huge amounts for signed shirts to support a good cause. Before I spoke, the master of ceremonies kicked off the evening and, within a minute or so, managed to tell a joke about a world famous fashion designer who had hanged himself a few days before. Most of us were embarrassed, and the shift in mood was palpable. According to the gospels, however, a fair number of those who passed by the foot of a cross that held a bruised and broken body found the scene hilarious (Mark 15:29–32). They derided and mocked the failed prophet, and there was cruelty in their laughter. In *Messiah*, Handel makes their laughter grow from an awkward titter to a blatant guffaw. The jeering moves from *hee! hee! hee!* to *ha! ha! ha!* and the One 'who is close to the Father's heart' (John 1:18) becomes 'the laughing stock of all my people' (Lam. 3:14). Some forms of laughter are simply inappropriate when they mask or convey malice, abuse, contempt or hatred – a fact mysteriously ignored by some of the greatest Christian theologians when they assured believers that one of the joys of heaven would be to gaze on the excruciating tortures of the damned.[4]

Added to this fact is the sincere conviction of some Christians who are not even at ease with happy or gentle laughter. They wonder if it has any place in a world where there is so much injustice, evil and suffering, and opt instead for sobriety in this vale of tears. I intend to deal with this difficulty later but this is the right moment to acknowledge that it points us to the paradox at the heart of Christianity. On the one hand it is manifestly a religion of joy – 'Rejoice in the Lord always, and again I say rejoice' (Phil. 4:4) – yet on the other, the same apostle Paul can write: 'I have unceasing anguish in my heart' (Rom. 9:2). He seems to recognise the dilemma of discipleship: we are 'sorrowful but always rejoicing' (2 Cor. 6:10), bound to One who is scoffed at but also messengers of 'the good news of Christ' (2 Cor. 10:14).

The paradox is not always appreciated, or even acknowledged, and in consequence the scriptures come to us lop-sided. Theologians and scholars point out that the Jesus of the New Testament is shown weeping, but never laughing; his mother shares the same state. On this view, a grim Galilean preacher makes the world grow grey with his breath and the Virgin Mary seems bereft of even the faintest smile. It is certainly the case that the Western imagination has been dominated by 'the man of sorrows' and it is no less true that much devotional art and iconography depict Mary in the doldrums. Are we being asked to see her as someone who has risen above her humanity (and therefore has no need to laugh), or is she actually one of us? Only a joke it seems can address the mystery.

A deeply devout woman, who has spent much of her life praying to Mary, dies and goes to heaven. She is granted a special favour by St Peter as a reward for her spiritual labours and she requests that she might put one question, just one question, to the mother of Jesus. Mary comes to her and the woman asks: 'Why is it that you never smile in all your pictures?' Mary pauses, and replies: 'I really wanted a girl!'

Jokes amuse me less than they used to but I love this one for its pathos, insight and surprise. It is a touching reminder that, before the many accolades and titles that are bestowed upon her later, Mary is presented in the New Testament as a human being sharing the joys and sorrows of a precarious world. Paul never discusses Mary in his letters to emerging Christian communities, and refers simply to the truth that Jesus had been born of a woman (Gal. 4:4). In bearing Jesus, Mary has to watch him grow and grow away from her to fulfil a destiny that will pierce her heart (Luke 2:35). She is a poignant figure in the gospels, observing her son from the sidelines, joining in the celebration at the marriage at Cana in Galilee and finally standing at the foot of the cross, a silent witness as others laugh. There must have been times when the attachment and intimacy of a daughter seemed preferable to the distant son she nurtured and loved. The Irish poet W. B. Yeats captures such inner turmoil in his 'Mother of God':

> What is this flesh I purchased with my pains
> This fallen star my milk sustains,
> This love that makes my heart's blood stop
> Or strikes a sudden chill into my bones
> And bids my hair stand up?[5]

Mary has to learn patience – such is the message of her life – and she inculcates in us the same discipline. Devotion to a person, a principle, an ideal, is a costly business that trades in tears. But surely she also smiles and laughs? A redeeming feature of Mel Gibson's otherwise harrowing and brutal film, *The Passion of Christ*, is a brief flashback that shows Mary chasing her young son around the kitchen table at Nazareth. A domestic scene known to every loving parent is transformed as Jesus and his mother are caught up in a moment of happiness. Her smile is radiant.

With the passage of time I have come to value Mary more. I light a candle before her icon most mornings in church and sometimes find myself sitting in silence before it at the end of long days. She is not smiling but there is a composure and knowingness in her countenance that puts me at ease. I think occasionally about the extraordinary impact of her life on the development of Christianity and muse on some of the strange doctrines and worldly practices perpetrated in her name. I tell myself that she would surely giggle at the popular (and preposterous) belief, condemned at the Council of Lyons in the ninth century, that since Christ, the Word of God, was conceived through the ear of Mary, he was also delivered through her ear. A strange nativity indeed, derived from the hearing of Gabriel's message at the Annunciation and biblical texts ignorantly wrenched out of context.

The politics and power struggles that attend Mary's status in the early centuries also reveal that the humble maiden standing rapt before the angel at Nazareth is far removed from the exalted figure that emerges in the fifth century. Her titles multiply and she becomes variously the bearer of God, 'the holy ornament of all the universe, the unquenchable lamp, the crown of virginity, the sceptre, the container of the uncontainable'[6]. Not all ecclesiastical parties are happy at the title of *theotokos* (God bearer) being conferred upon Mary: one opponent, Nestor, a Syrian monk of formidable scholarship, prefers *Christotokos* (bearer of Christ), and he conducts a propaganda campaign accompanied by bully boys who take the fight to the streets. Nestor is physically attacked by the abbot of the White Monastery at Atripe for his impertinent and unorthodox theology. To make absolutely sure that Nestor's party does not fight back and there is no backsliding on Mary as *theotokos,* Cyril, bishop of Alexan-

dria, drafts a memo to his supporters in Constantinople accompanied by 'sweeteners' for ladies-in-waiting and eunuchs at the
imperial court. The details have come down to us:

> 77,760 gold pieces, twenty-four carpets, twenty-five woollen
> tapestries, twenty-four silken veils, twenty-eight cushions,
> thirty-six throne covers, tapestries and carpets, ivory stools,
> Persian drapery and ostrich eggs.[7]

Cyril achieves his ambition. Nestor ends his days in exile. I can only
smile at such shenanigans. I look again at Mary's icon, a little more
closely than usual. The same poise and serenity are evident as the
child Jesus rests in her arms. But she is not actually gazing at him.
Her face is set towards the beholder, so momentarily we are one in
our wry contemplation of her astonishing transition from handmaid
to Mother of God.[8] And in this moment I am content in my own
mind that her time on earth included days of ease and laughter
before an imperial Church incorporated her into 'the most solemn
formulations of a Christian system and over the next century a
central marker of Christian identity'[9]. The days when she saw Jesus
laughing and joking in the presence of friends – this young, attractive
and curious man, eager and energetic for the new project of the
kingdom and amusing his listeners as he tells fantastic stories in
order to make his point. This convivial man as he dines with bad
company, and captivates Mary at his feet by his vivacity as Martha
scuttles about in the kitchen worrying about greasy spoons instead
of sharing the spell of the moment. This ample man who enjoys food
and wine, delights in table talk and takes little children in his arms as
he shares with them the deeper secrets of life that so easily pass
unremarkable adults by. This is no severe saviour scorching the earth
with the fire of his gospel. It is the storyteller and healer who knows
'there is a time to laugh' (Eccles. 3:4) that banishes misery from the
human heart, and anticipates a promised age without sin or death,
when 'our mouth will be filled with laughter, and our tongue with
shouts of joy' (Ps. 126:2).

   This, it seems to me, is the best answer to the unyielding pessimism I spoke of earlier that construes the world as an extended
Passion narrative, a place more akin to a hospital or asylum given the

prevalence of suffering and pain. Both images are real, but not to the extent that they should deflect us from a deeper and more enabling truth. Life before the Last Day offers a peculiar freedom to celebrate the laughter and humour that refuse to give sourness, cynicism or despair the final word concerning what it means to be human. Tragedy and scepticism can be found in the writings of the Hebrew prophets, in Lamentations, Job and Ecclesiastes, but it is also worth remembering that the New Israel which is the Church remains faithful to the God of Abraham, of Isaac and of Jacob.

Isaac, we recall from an earlier chapter, means 'laughter'. The name is chosen by God and conferred at a key moment during the establishment of the Covenant. Abraham, who will be Isaac's father, will become the father of many nations, and Isaac will partake of an everlasting covenant. This is the biggest of deals. Abraham is already steeped in years – he will be a hundred years old by the time Isaac is born. His wife, Sarah, is already ninety, yet her shrivelled form will bring forth for him a son. God's promise and its fulfilment cause both of them to laugh; neither can believe their miraculous fortune (Gen. 17:17; 21:6–7) and their laughter arises from a joyful wonder and trust in Providence[10]. Their child will be well named.

This scriptural insight – that by virtue of a name, laughter is inscribed into our relationship with God – gives weight to the divine promise that we shall not be overcome whatever the circumstances. Laughter is part of our 'clothing for the soul divine'. Along with the face of Jesus and the illumination provided by the Spirit it assures us that in the end we shall be safe. I am aware that some eminent authors did not subscribe wholeheartedly to this view. No less a figure than St Jerome interpreted Sarah's laughter as a kind of faithless scoffing. St John Chrysostom pointed out that Sarah was rebuked for her laughter, and that saints, including Paul, never laughed 'except in defiance of imminent martyrdom'[11].

I find this a strange doctrine. It robs religion of its vitality and joy and humanity of its innate capacity for humour. We are born for more than repentance and I am very glad that, along with the 'sobersides' and curmudgeons of the Christian tradition, we can find the holy fools who cast the familiar in a new light through their rejection of worldly standards. At theological college I had a part in a play about St Francis of Assisi. The script was not exactly Shakespearean and it included several songs. Not quite *Francis – The Musical*, but a jaunty romp through a racy life that ignored religious conventions and sought the 'more excellent way' (1 Cor. 12:31). We brought a degree of panache to the text and lyrics but I managed to drive the producer to distraction by my lack of co-ordination – my inability in the last act to move my hands at the same time and in the same direction as the rest of the cast as they made a choreographed response to the beauty of creation. Their hands were lifted high in praise of the sun but mine inexplicably seemed marooned as they lagged behind, unsure of their intended destination. It was painful and hilarious to behold this spectacle at the rehearsals, surpassed only by the Oxfam tea cosy on my head that served as a bishop's mitre. It was this headgear apparently that stopped my New Testament professor from taking the show seriously when she attended the first night! Francis, I am convinced, would not have been offended by any of this. He described his followers as *ioculatores Domini* – jokers and jesters of God. By the way in which we took liberty with some of the more risible lines in the play, along with my lack of theatrical finesse at the finale, we qualified as his brothers and sisters. Our audience laughed and no one took themselves too seriously. A college play fostered lasting friendships and memories that have survived the attrition of the years, and taught us a little concerning the meaning of salvation. In its occasional absurdities, unintended puns but, most of all, its genuine concern to depict a rather beautiful life untrammelled by status or ambition (except for the great causes of the kingdom and the poor), it associated laughter with 'the lineaments of the risen Christ'[12] and humour as part of what is most endearing in our nature.

This last truth is also embodied in the life of another of my theological heroes, the great Reformer Martin Luther. During my ministerial training it was his courage and passion and his approach to theology as the deepest form of engagement with life's questions that impressed me. Following a recent invitation to review a book by sixteen church historians that examines Luther not as Reformer or theologian but as *pastor*, I have become more aware of just how integral humour was to his thought and life.[13] Next to his work as monk, scholar and professor in the lecture hall, more of his daily life in the small town of Wittenberg was occupied with pastoral duties than anything else. He baptised, visited the sick, preached (oh, how he preached!) instructed the young and comforted the dying, even holding them in his arms. His break with Rome and his most famous work, the Ninety Five Theses of 31 October 1517, make us overlook the fact that he remained a preacher and pastor in Wittenberg until his death in 1546. Whatever else he was doing or embroiled in, he was at the same time the people's shepherd. In the pulpit he spoke to them of the cross, but earthy humour peppered his sermons. When a congregation seemed unresponsive he would liken preaching 'to singing in the woods where all one hears is the echo of one's voice!' For Luther, God laughs, and so Christ 'is a pauper, a poor donkey rider seated on a borrowed animal' confounding the expectations of the orthodox who were looking for a king. It's all so topsy-turvy, this business of the gospel, and he wanted his hearers to get the joke that King Jesus prefers a beast of burden to great castles and worldly pomp. The preacher at Wittenberg was never afraid to 'play the fool'. His delight in the sensual – pictures, music, food and the love of a good woman – accompanied him in the pulpit. He fed his congregation on images of farmhands, maids and even beer barrels! The sublime was mediated through home, hearth and field so that 'girls of sixteen, old folks and peasants' could smile as well as be astonished by the glory of the Father in their midst. Even when Luther pointed them to the suffering of the crucified, he revealed the deep humanity of Christ – the one 'with holes in hands, feet and side; the God who has come near to us, into the midst of our twisted and ruined existence'.

It's worth re-reading this last sentence before moving on. It defines much of Luther's world. For all his ability to laugh, he was also a serious man on a serious earth, immersed in the great disruptions of his day and deeply conscious of the waywardness of human nature. And like the rest of us he had to contend with his own human frailties. In this respect, he was sometimes over-scrupulous in the confession of his sins and occasionally morbidly preoccupied with the minor blemishes that shape our humanity. It's a shame that the following verse had not been written at the time; it would have put things in perspective in the confessional and probably made him less anxious:

Once in a saintly passion
I cried with desperate grief,
'O Lord my heart is black with guile,
Of sinners I am chief.'
Then stopped my guardian angel
And whispered from behind:
'Vanity, my little man,
You're nothing of the kind.'[14]

Outside of the confessional, humour helped Luther to cope with
depression and a range of health problems. In addition to leading a
reform movement that placed his life in danger and keeping several
secretaries busy with his writings, he suffered from stomach disor-
ders, gall stones, headaches and a deteriorating heart condition (he
died of *angina pectoris* at 63). But his wit and colourful invective kept
him going. He likened his ailments to the image of Satan riding
through his head, looking for a resting place: 'I resist the devil and it
is often with a fart that I chase him away.' As far as I am aware, such a
direct and pungent approach to the problem of evil is not to be found
anywhere else in scripture or church history! Luther learned from
his studies that we are at our best as human beings when we get
ourselves off our hands and depend only on that source of righteous-
ness and truth which is not of our own making. He counselled his
listeners to think lightly of themselves: life between the first and
second advents of Christ was a form of carnival. And when enemies
of Christ seemed to prevail they were to be laughed at and mocked.
Writing against the scandalous practice of indulgences that
extracted money from the poor in return for the remission of time
spent in Purgatory, he listed newly-discovered holy relics for Archbishop Albrecht of Mainz to add to his dubious collection. They
included:

Three flames from the burning bush on Mount Sinai;
two feathers and an egg from the Holy Spirit;
a remnant of the flag with which Christ opened hell, a large
lock of Beelzebub's beard stuck on the same flag;
one half of the archangel Gabriel's wing:

five nice, shiny strings from the harp of David and three beautiful locks of Absalom's hair, which got caught in the oak and left him hanging.[15]

The Pope was not amused by such satirical and withering banter but despite threats and censure from Rome, Luther carried on. Worship, a wife and children, enjoying bowls and music and playing with his dog Tolpel preserved his sanity. Ripe language, deadpan humour and his spiritual insouciance fortified him in his darker moments and kept him humble:

> I ask that people make no reference to my name; let them call themselves Christians, not Lutherans. What is Luther? After all, the teaching is not mine, neither was I crucified for anyone ...
> I have often said I am like a ripe stool and the world's like a gigantic anus and we're about to let go of each other. I thank you, dear God, that you allow me to stay in your little flock that suffers persecution for the sake of your Word.[16]

Other spiritual writers have used scatological images[17] to make their point but few I suspect have managed to combine stool, anus and God in a short passage that for all its earthiness can still touch rather than offend. Luther wanted men and women to stay true to the Word, but he also wanted them to laugh at what he saw 'as ugliness and error within the Church'[18]. His rude jibes and scandalous jests aimed to correct the corruptions of earthly power gone wrong and reform an institution that had, for too long, fallen tragically short of its highest ideals. At table with family and friends he was no less irreverent, for to be faithful to Christ was to enjoy the privilege of a free man. Unburdened by the sorrows of time's passing, and convinced of another order of things that transcended sin and mortality, he remained hopeful. On his death bed he knew himself 'to be a beggar, that's a fact'. But he also knew that even if 'the world would end tomorrow I would still plant a little apple tree today'[19]. This saying appeared in Germany in the aftermath of World War II, and was attributed to Luther because it sounded just like him! And so it does: it is the Wittenberg pastor, speaking here to believers who have to smile at the prospect of an apple seed taking root in the most unpromising of circumstances. By the sheer incongruity of the image they are, in some mysterious way, saved. They are urged to arrange the present well and persevere. They should laugh and take nothing too seriously except their need of God, the duty of prayer and the fulfilling of 'God's commands to care for the world around us'[20]. More than five centuries later, the image and the teaching retain their power.

Notes

[1] Augustine, *City of God,* Book 15, pp. 15, 21.

[2] Published in 1895, the novel consists of twelve letters written by J. Stark Munro to a friend and former fellow-student Herbert Swanborough, of Lowell, Massachusetts, between 1881–1884.

[3] This tendency can be traced back to Aristotle who wrote that 'no animal laughs save Man'. His treatise *On the Parts of Animals,* x. 29.

[4] See Thomas Aquinas, *Summa Theologica,* III, Suppl. qu. 94. art. 1, and Peter Lombard, *Sententiae,* IV, dist. 5, 9. Both cited in F. W. Farrar, *Eternal Hope* (London, 1892), p. 66.

[5] W. B. Yeats, *The Collected Poems of W. B. Yeats* (London, 1933), pp. 281–282.

[6] Cited in the canons of the Council of Ephesus, Pentecost 431, by Gregory, *Vox Populi,* p. 105.

[7] John I. McEnerney (trans.), *Letters 1–110, St Cyril of Alexandria* (Washington, 1987), pp. 151–152.

[8] A more detailed account of Mary as *theotokos* and the Council of Ephesus 431 can be found in Miri Rubin, *Mother of God: A History of the Virgin Mary* (Allen Lane, 2009), pp. 43–49.

[9] Rubin, *Mother of God,* p. 43.

[10] Between the two joyful accounts there is another story in Genesis where Sarah laughs to herself when she overhears a messenger from God telling Abraham that she will bear a son in old age. In this instance she appears to doubt the promise. Later she denies that she laughed and is rebuked by God (Genesis 18:9–15).

[11] Peter L. Berger, *Redeeming Laughter: The Comic Dimension of Human Experience* (Walter de Gruyter, 1997), p. 198.

[12] Peter Brown, *The Body and Society* (Faber & Faber, 1989), p. 442.

[13] Timothy J. Wengert (ed.), *The Pastoral Luther: Essays on Martin Luther's Practical Theology* (Eerdmans, 2009).

[14] F. C. Happold, *Prayer and Meditation* (Pelican, 1971), p. 105.

[15] Wengert, *Pastoral Luther*, p. 97.

[16] Wengert, *Pastoral Luther*, p. 89.

[17] See M. A. Screech, *Laughter at the Foot of the Cross* (Penguin Books, 1997), pp. 234–239, on the writings of the Benedictine monk, scholar and humanist, Rabelais (1494–1553).

[18] Screech, *Laughter*, p. 9.

[19] Wengert, *Pastoral Luther*, p. 89.

[20] Wengert, *Pastoral Luther*, p. 38.

CHAPTER 8

Hold Everything Dear

Luther would be amused, surprised and, I suspect, rather pleased by what I'm about to share with you. First, it would be possible, even at a distance, to hear his laughter as he contemplated the surreal transformation of the town square in Wittenberg. Currently, the statue of the reformer is being renovated and in its place the artist Ottmar Hörl has filled the square with 800 plastic statuettes of Luther. They are based on the statue under repair and are painted in vivid colours. Hörl has named his installation *Martin Luther – I'm Standing Here* and it is an astonishing sight. Luther is literally everywhere to be seen, each figure identical to the other, the mouth set firmly and both hands clasping his translation of the New Testament. The humble pastor, who once tended his little flock and wanted people to call themselves Christians not Lutherans, has been reconfigured into an icon of the Western Church, revered by Protestants and, increasingly, rediscovered by Roman Catholic scholars and theologians.[1] Luther abides, with his 800 pairs of feet planted firmly on the solid ground that was once the heartbeat of the European Reformation. It's a scene without parallel and, if we allow for the lapse of time, one that Luther would have recounted over meals with friends, no doubt embellishing the details as he went along whilst roaring at the sheer unpredictability of it all!

The second fact I have to relate also has to do with planting. A few months before Hörl's installation, representatives of different Christian denominations gathered in the Lutergarten (Luther's Garden) on the banks of the Elbe in Wittenberg. Anglicans, Methodists, Lutherans, Roman Catholics and Orthodox came together to plant 500 trees as a symbol of the global influence of the Reformation and as a sign of reconciliation between the various branches of Christianity. Luther would be delighted by the gesture, and in particular its origin: the idea of the garden was inspired by his own declaration that he would still plant a little apple tree even if everything ended tomorrow.

The potency of the image is not surprising. Trees are our gracious companions and we spend many intimate hours in their presence. They dignify and sustain the planet and are far more valuable than lazy minds imagine. The Californian Department of Forestry and Fire Protection has calculated that a single tree living for fifty years will contribute service worth more than 200,000 dollars to the community during its lifetime. This includes providing oxygen, recycling water, regulating humidity, controlling air pollution, producing protein, providing shelter for wildlife, controlling land erosion and fertilising the soil.[2] Luther was remarkably prescient in this respect. Soaked in scripture, he knew that we should not 'damage the earth, or the sea or the trees' (Rev. 7:3). And, in his own words, he realised that every tree is precious, 'far more glorious than if it were made of gold and silver'. I need no convincing of this truth. A stone's throw from where I am writing these words stands a tree of such magnificence that I invariably pause as I walk past it as a means of conveying my respect and gratitude. Its vast extended branches dominate the surrounding space rather like the statuettes in the Wittenberg square. In the dusk its formidable trunk appears to me as the stuff of fairy tales and I half-expect elves and goblins to emerge from its secret lair.

In our vicarage garden we have an apple tree of no particular beauty that has survived many gales. The birds take refuge there and, each Autumn, it yields its fruit. Sometimes we can hardly keep pace and its gifts fall unceremoniously to the ground. Eventually we gather them up and there is the promise of pastries to come, provided we do not squander our pickings. Soon enough cold winds will strip its branches bare, but it will come again with the certainty of Spring. In his journals recording his two years and two months near the woods by Walden Pond Massachusetts, Henry David Thoreau noted that he 'frequently tramped eight or ten miles through the deepest snow to keep an appointment with a beech tree, or a yellow birch, or an old acquaintance among the pines'[3]. No sentimentalist in relation to a natural order where teeming forms of life suffered and preyed on one another, Thoreau seems nevertheless to have approached trees in a spirit of reverence, seeing in them a silent riddle or secret that contained a clue to his own spiritual life. Wisdom from a quite different mystical tradition came to the same conclusion:

> Think of a tree. When you think of a tree, you tend to think of a distinctly defined object; and on a certain level, it is. But when you look more closely at the tree, you will see that ultimately it has no independent existence. When you contemplate it, you will find that it dissolves into an extremely subtle net of relationships that stretches across the universe. The rain that falls on its leaves, the wind that sways it, the soil that nourishes and sustains it, all the seasons and the weather, moonlight and starlight and sunlight – all form part of this tree. As you begin to think about the tree more and more, you will discover that everything in the universe helps to make a tree what it is, that it cannot at any moment be isolated from anything else, and that at every moment its nature is subtly changing.[4]

This quotation resonates for a number of reasons. It encourages mindfulness – that particular and deep form of attention to living things which grasps that there is nothing ordinary or unremarkable under the sun. In the woods Thoreau found a whole universe in an 'insect crawling amid the pine needles on the forest floor and endeavouring to conceal itself from my sight'[5]. Meanwhile, the upright citizens of Concord – the nearby town he had left to experience solitude and nature – went about their daily business 'sound asleep nearly half their time'[6]. It reminds us that, subtly or otherwise, change defines the surface of things, however much we crave the consistencies of habit and routine. Most of all, it is an affirmation of the interconnectedness of everything. Nothing exists independently of anything else. A tree is a discreet convergence of diffuse energies – sun, soil, star and seasons. And a wood or forest with its intricacy of crossing paths – the strange and fleeting marriage of birds, insects, seeds, spores, ferns, worms and lichen – serves as a metaphor for all reality. Reality is what Thoreau sought in the woods of Walden. As he experienced the passage of time and seasons, and 'the sympathy of Nature ... with our race'[7], it became

ever more clear that he should have 'intelligence with the earth ...',
for 'am I not partly leaves and vegetable mould myself?'[8]

The teaching here is that we should hold everything dear, should
clothe ourselves with the heavens and crown ourselves with the
stars, because we are part of a singular whole. The creation narrative
in the opening chapter of Genesis testifies to the same truth: humankind and animals are created on the same day (the sixth day) and both
alike are given the fruit of trees and 'every green plant' as their
means of sustenance (Gen. 1:29–30). Their creator directs them to
the same table and they are nourished by the same food. Without
exception or reminder, everything 'that has the breath of life' is
provided for and where the individual elements of creation are seen
as 'good' (for e.g. Gen. 1:4, 10) the whole is *very good* (Gen. 1:31),
perfectly corresponding to the divine intention. Existence under
God, properly understood, entails not separation but unity and
communion.

To view the world in this way is to choose to live with compassion.
The lives of others, the well-being of creatures and the care of
flowers, plants and trees, all assume a power of meaning that call for
our allegiance, respect and commitment. To recognise that everything that lives is in some sense sacred is a key to the rationality and
unity of an ordered world and a summons to action when life in
whatever form is threatened or justice denied. Interconnectedness
amounts to more than instantaneous global communication, or the
economic interplay between the local and the global. In terms of
how we ought to live it is part of the ethical impulse that fuels our
desire to do no evil and, wherever possible, promote the good. It is
best thought of as a world view or a way of life and, increasingly in a
hollow consumerist culture, it has a human face and dedicated
followers.

Until very recently, I was unfamiliar with the revered Vietnamese
Zen master, Thich Nhat Hahn, in his eighties still one of the world's
most influential Buddhist leaders. He is the guiding light behind *The
Order of Interbeing*, a movement of disciples across the world with
monasteries in France, America, Germany, Australia, Thailand, Indo-
nesia and Hong Kong.[9] As a monk, he requires followers to engage in
meditation and silence. As they eat, they consider each mouthful

carefully, reflecting on how much they consume, its provenance and the ethical implications of eating it. Thich Nhat Hanh does not equivocate on such issues:

> UNESCO reports that every day 40,000 children die because they do not have enough food. Meanwhile many of us eat a lot of meat and drink a lot of alcohol. In order to make a piece of meat you have to use a lot of cereal and grain and that grain could be used to feed dying children. So eating that meat is akin to eating the flesh of your own son. We should eat in such a way that conserves our compassion.[10]

With the rise of the Green Movement some will interpret this message as a passing fad, except in this case it happens to be delivered by a well-meaning but naïve eco-crusader in a monk's robe. They would be wrong. His book on ecology, *The World We Have*, has become a best-seller but his roots go much deeper than our contemporary concerns for the environment. He opposed the South Vietnamese government during the Vietnam War and risked his life in the jungle to assist bombed villagers. His opposition to that conflict led to his exile from his homeland for forty years. His work for peace influenced Martin Luther King, who subsequently nominated him for the Nobel Peace Prize. In the 1970s, when Vietnamese and Cambodian refugees boarded overcrowded boats to escape persecution, Thich Nhat Hanh spent months crossing the South China Sea saving lives.

When he was finally allowed to return to Vietnam in 2005, thousands attended the retreats he organised. So many followers joined his order that the Communist authorities ordered a crackdown, frightened by his influence. Many of those persecuted monks left the country or now live in hiding. It is an impressive record of a long life dedicated to prayer, simplicity, compassion and a profound respect for the earth and the essential unity of all natural phenomena. It is a spiritual vision of the world, with intimations of Genesis and the life of principle that led Thoreau into the woods in search of a higher wisdom. Separated by two centuries, both men march to the same music. They sing a hymn to the universe and grasp that the essential point is not to inspect the world but behold it. From this perspective flows the ethics and right actions that promote personal virtue and safeguard human flourishing.

By his own estimation, Thoreau was 'a mystic, Transcendentalist[11] and a natural philosopher'. To these important categories we should also add the shining light of a social conscience. He was a man who possessed tutored moral sense, and even *knowing* about evil made him feel an accessory to the crime. At a personal level he refused to connive with practices that he knew to be inhumane. As a young man out of Harvard College he was offered and accepted a decent job teaching in the public school at Concord, where he had once been a student. It lasted only two weeks. He resigned when the school committee instructed him to use corporal punishment on his students. In July 1846, he was arrested and put in jail for not having paid his poll tax. It was the briefest of imprisonments but his refusal to pay stemmed from an even deeper refusal to recognise the power of a government 'which buys and sells, men, women and children, like cattle at the door of its senate house'[12]. He was referring, of course, to black slavery, and his pen produced three powerful essays[13] on the issue that were to influence later generations. Mahatma Gandhi linked the essay 'Civil Disobedience' with non-violent resistance in Africa and India. Martin Luther King Jr frequently cited it during the civil rights movement in 1960s America, as did the campaigners who protested against the war in Vietnam. The essay extended Thoreau's fame a century after his death, and for a time he was reinvented as a social activist – a role largely engineered by well-meaning enthusiasts in search of a voice to represent their course. His face was to be found on posters and sweatshirts but, in truth, he was not a social reformer: he was suspicious of 'do gooding' and in *Walden* he noted that: 'If I knew for certainty that a man was coming to my house with the conscious design of doing me good, I should run for my life'[14]. A sane choice, I'm bound to add. Thoreau did not poke or meddle in other people's lives and he asked for the same respect. What he did, however, as he lived simply and frugally, was to cultivate his moral imagination and make important connections. Because heaven was under his feet as well as over his head, he came to see and believe in a power – a higher law – that permeated everything. To this he gave the name Love. It informed the habits of his heart and convinced him that 'no humane being ... will wantonly murder any creature', and that furthermore 'the hare in its extremity cries like a child'[15]. This recognition of the transcendental unity of things led him not only to the self-reliance that would not raise a hand to the robin or mouse that shared his world at Walden Pond; it also required him to assert the truth of his heart over the laws on the statute books. Going to jail or resisting taxation constituted peaceable means of thwarting unjust systems of government and bringing about change.

We are more than halfway through this chapter. It's time to draw out the implications of what it means to hold everything dear and to believe that the sensual world and the imperatives of conscience are, in some mysterious way, related. Several things occur to me, all of which have some bearing on our understanding of redemption. Thoreau and Thich Nhat Hanh encourage in us a deeper love of the natural world, a pristine vision of creation informed by prayer and silence and that humble form of attention to the divine in all things. We find it easy to honour such sentiments with our lips – to sing 'Morning has broken like the first morning' with gusto, without necessarily engaging our eyes or hearts. More conscious of the world's sorrows and the dying of the light, we find it hard to burn with expectation or be thrilled by the friendship of the turning year as the seasons unfold. Mindfulness – 'the discipline of looking always at what is to be seen'[16] (or for that matter touched or tasted) – reclothes us and awakens us to the trace of the eternal when everything is one. Nature has many shrines and they hark back to Genesis and the creation of an earth that was 'very good'.

Because it is a discipline, mindfulness has to be learned, embedded in our lives and even fought for in an age that understands little concerning the obligations of a genuinely spiritual life or the need for solitude. And there is the problem of time. Few of us can sit undisturbed in our doorways from sunrise until noon amidst the pines[17], but if our desire goes deep enough we can make the space where our vision is restored and we are summoned once again to a more compassionate engagement with life. Desire leads us to prayer, to the stillness and quiet that call for the surrender of our talkative selves. In the following passage, John Austin Baker points us to the work of intercession. He is primarily concerned with the lives of others, but such concern extends naturally and properly to the whole created order:

> Once we have grasped clearly what we are doing when we pray
> for others, we shall see that the most important requirement by
> far is inner calmness and tranquillity. We are not engaged in
> creating or producing anything, but in becoming aware of what
> is already the fact, namely that God is immediately and inti-
> mately present both to ourselves and to the ones for whom we
> are praying. Our task is to hold the awareness of this fact in the
> still centre of our being, to unite our love for them with God's
> love, in the quiet but total confidence that he will use our love
> to help bring about the good in them which we both desire. In
> technical terms, therefore, intercession is a form of that kind of
> prayer known as 'contemplation', with the special feature that
> here we contemplate not God himself but God in his relation-
> ship of love towards those whom we also love; and on the basis
> of our partnership with him we entrust our love into his hands
> to be used in harness with his own for their benefit.[18]

Almost every line in this extract merits further comment or appreciation. At its heart is the mindfulness that transcends our immediate
or selfish concerns, increases our awareness of the real beyond our
own lives and rearranges the insides of our heads. Prayer is the home
of the imagination and dreams, and it is through the imagination that
we recognise ourselves at ease in a world of terrible beauty and
bitter tears. If we are sufficiently quiet and brave enough, we can also
hear the yearning of the heart to begin again, to delight in the dew
and rain and to stand with those who are burdened by the pain of
injustice. The glory of the dawn also belongs to them and, when we
recognise this, prayer becomes a form of resistance and mindfulness
a matter of taking sides.

I'm reminded here of E. M. Forster's novel, *Howards End*. Published in 1910, it deals with personal relationships and the clash of
values. On the one hand we have the Schlegel sisters, Margaret and
Helen, and their brother Tibby. They care deeply about high ideals,
the possibilities of civilised living, music, literature, conversation
and the bonds of friendship. On the other stand the Wilcoxes, Henry
and his children Charles, Paul and Evie – a family wedded to
business, money, practicalities and transactions on the Stock
Exchange. They are suspicious of emotions and imagination and
confine themselves to the facts. To the consternation of both fami-

lies, Margaret marries Henry. Her love and sure purpose are tested
by strains and misunderstandings; the relationship falters, but does
not break. In the end, torn between her husband and her sister, she
manages to bridge the mistrust that separates them. Peace and
human dignity win out but not before we have been confronted with
the initial divide: the Schlegels worry about making the world fairer
while the Wilcoxes fret about their stocks and shares. The gulf is not
so wide that it cannot be traversed, but the text subtly explores the
choice between money and moral scruples, between being too
complacent concerning the way things are in the world and responding to the claims of conscience and the need for social change. To
oversimplify greatly, the book poses a question: am I a Schlegel or a
Wilcox? To practice mindfulness is to know unequivocally where we
stand on this question.[19]

To speak, as we have been doing, of the duty of resistance and the
necessity of taking sides is to be reminded that redemption is a
human as well as a divine activity. It is about grace and the loving
wisdom of God and, for many believers, it has always been primarily
about the experience of mercy, of being 'ransomed, healed,
restored, forgiven'. Such was the experience of Bunyan and many
other evangelical Christians who have testified to a religion of the
heart and a deep sense of blessed assurance. All of this stands, but
alongside it as a moral corollary must be emphasised the duty of
unceasing and costly work for the sake of the world. And this is
something *we do*, out of gratitude for what we have received but also
from necessity – from the disquiet within us that so many still weep,
and the determination that such affairs cannot continue. They grieve
our hearts, and to be duped by the love of money or to tolerate
injustice constitute forms of betrayal to the author of all good things.
So we work and pray, not only to be delivered from temptation or to
present clean hands and a pure heart before the altar of God. We act
in order that salvation might ease the pitilessness of the planet and
restore the innocence and wonder that belong to a redeemed
humanity. We commit because we must: our love of Christ and our
sense of ourselves in the here and now of a skewed moral universe
leave us no choice.

A conclusion begs to be drawn at this point, and it is this: we are
partners with God in the work of redemption. The sirens that wail

down the street, the sickness that destroys in the noon day and the heel of a boot on someone's face, are not alien to our concerns and are not to be dismissed as the responsibilities of others. They are exactly our business. We act on God's behalf; we are God's helpers, we make things happen for the common good and, in such endeavours, we honour the divine name and further humanity. The Most High and the human are 'together bound', and God requires that each one of us should be with him and for him in an active partnership.

Another question emerges here: is this how we think of ourselves in relation to God and the extension of love's redeeming work? For me, the question has the same importance as the choice to be made between the Schlegel and Wilcox families. How we answer will say much concerning our understanding or ignorance of the ways in which the divine energies impinge upon our world. It will also make clearer the extent of the personal obligation we feel in relation to the horrors and assaults that stalk our earth and maim its children and their hopes of a future.

Behind the question, more or less hidden from sight, lurks a huge theological issue, indeed a debate that has marked and sometimes soured long Christian centuries. Both concern the issue of free will, and the extent to which imperfect human beings can genuinely do any good thing. Theological estimations have not always been flattering in this respect, and it is distressing to learn that important voices within the Christian tradition have portrayed humankind as little better than a worm or bubble, or a creature so hopelessly mired in sin that to speak of our capacity for goodness amounts to a contradiction in terms.[20] Other voices have countered such pessimism. St Bonaventura[21] developed a moral theology that represented a 'partly-partly' system: a process of collaboration between God and each individual man and woman. In his estimation, decent human endeavour relies 'partly on God's grace' for its initiation and increase, but also 'partly on the activity of free will'. Man's free will was not entirely lost at the Fall; it was weakened, certainly, but a residual, innate force remained which 'goads him towards the good and protects against the evil'. This gift and potential represented his *synderesis* – the energy that on the one hand denied he was bad to the bone and, on the other, asserted his capacity

to exercise free will in co-operation with the grace of God to secure
good ends. The theology which permits this creative partnership
came to be known as *synergism* and in the arena of human morality it
worked from the premise that God requires that each of us should be
his willing companion. It is a double blessing: God needs us and we
are morally capable of furthering his purposes. In prayer, as John
Austin Baker reminded us, it is partnership that allows our love to be
entrusted into the divine hands so that both loves can benefit the
lives of others. And it is St Paul who impresses on us that we are not
only the work of an almighty hand, but also God's helpers (Eph.
2:10). Remarkably, God's grace is assisted by our efforts. For the
good of our souls and the salvation of the world, we should all be
synergists now. It is not an easy term to remember but, once committed to heart and understood, it is capable of transforming our
understanding of what we can do and are expected to do in our time
in the name of justice and truth.

This notion of partnership with the divine, articulated so thought-
fully and humanely by Bonaventura, has its counterpart in Judaism.
Abraham Joshua Heschel asserted that it was God's dream to have
'humanity as a partner in the drama of continuous creation. By
whatever we do, by every act we carry out, we either advance or
obstruct the drama of redemption'[22]. As we might expect, there is a
shift in emphasis here away from the great cosmic drama of the cross
to the more prosaic but nevertheless hugely important role of the
individual – each righteous person who comes along and, bit by bit,
adds to the world's lustre. So it is that 'with each righteous act, the
world is perfected a bit more, and for God, the world becomes more
important'[23]. Two big claims are being advanced here. First, that
God is affected by what we do – something that is entirely in keeping
with the passionate God of the Hebrew scriptures who weeps over
his people's failings and delights in their pursuit of holiness (for e.g.
Isa. 2:1–3). Second, redemption is interpreted as a continuing and
piecemeal undertaking – a work that is always in progress and
seeking to fulfil the scriptural mandate to be active in the pursuit of
righteousness. To do good is not only to seek peace for ourselves but
also to pursue it in other places as well (Ps. 34:14).

Jewish wisdom urges synergists (ourselves as God's partners) to
engage in a process of 'repairing the world'. It has a theological term

for this task (mentioned only in passing in Chapter 1), one so important that for some it has come to represent the reason for their existence on earth. To hold everything dear is to engage in the process of *tikkun olam,* fixing the world 'piece by piece, peace by peace'. Slowly, precariously and often in the aftermath of setbacks and disillusionment, we are called to repair what is broken, drawing strength from our love of the world and the recognition of its beauty and fragility as the handiwork of God (Exod. 19:5). Mark L. Winer, Senior Rabbi at the West London Synagogue, has written movingly and passionately of what it means to honour the precept of *tikkun olam* at a time when prodigious energies are destroying the earth rather than sustaining it:

> Tikkun olam is the expression of justice, compassion and mercy in fostering the reconciliation of Shiites, Sunnis and Kurds within Iraq. Tikkun olam means a Marshall Plan for Iraq to rebuild its hospitals, schools and public services. Tikkun olam means the West's acknowledgement of Arab humiliation and the establishment of a mutual respect among Christian Jews and our Abrahamic sibling Muslims.[24]

He writes as a religious Zionist who recognises that Israel has done too little to promote mutual respect in the Holy Land and too much that continues to humiliate and impoverish Palestinians. But his pen and his passion are also fuelled by a lifetime's experience of racial segregation in the United States, close co-operation with devout black and white Christians and the conviction (based on long years of a principled social activism) that the 'shattered urn'[25] of the world can be put together again: 'Who could imagine fifty years ago that we might overturn racial segregation in the American South? Who could envision fifty years ago driving a car from Paris to Berlin, crossing the German border without even a passport check, with only a sign welcoming us to Germany?'[26]

It is possible to see in such work and witness and, no less, in the turning of a world that sometimes, against all the odds, moves away from political darkness back into light, the strength and enduring power of deep theological truths. Redemption, understood as the duty and joy of holding the world dear[27], is something we undertake in partnership with God and all friends of God. Synergists move beyond religious boundaries and learn from others. Trees concern us, beginning with the one forever associated with Calvary and extending to every glorious tree that now adorns and sustains our common life.[28] Redemption is our sacred task in the midst of global discontent and calls for our commitment to wholeness[29] and our willingness to engage in *tikkun olam*. In part, this is what our hours and days are for: the graced opportunities to repair the world, piece by piece, peace by peace.

Notes

[1] In 2009 a conference was convened in Augsburg to celebrate the tenth anniversary of the signing of a joint declaration between the Roman Catholic Church and Lutheran churches which resolved a long-standing dispute concerning the theology of justification. Justification concerns the means whereby a believer is made righteous in the sight of God and the acrimonious debate over when and how this occurred had long been a divisive issue between the respective Christian traditions.

[2] See 'Sacred Trees', www.dennydavis.net/poemfiles/trees.hton for breakdown of yield.

[3] Henry David Thoreau, *Walden* (Fall River Press, 2008 edition).

[4] Attributed to Sogyal Rinpoche, *The Tibetan Book of Living and Dying*.

[5] Thoreau, *Walden*, p. 312.

[6] Thoreau, *Walden*, p.312.

[7] Thoreau, *Walden*, p. 131.

[8] Thoreau, *Walden*, p. 131.

[9] For more information go to www.mindfulnessretreats.org.uk.

[10] Part of interview 'Monk on a Mission', *The Independent*, 10 August 2010.

[11] The Transcendentalists were an eclectic group of New England writers and thinkers during the 1830s and 1840s that included Ralph Waldo Emerson and Margaret Fuller.

[12] Henry David Thoreau, *Walden and Civil Disobedience* (Penguin Classics, 1986), p. 30.

[13] 'Civil Disobedience' (1849), 'Slavery in Massachusetts' (1854), and 'A Plea for Captain John Brown' (1859).

[14] *Walden Thoreau*, p. 13.

[15] Thoreau, *Walden*, p.201.

[16] Thoreau, *Walden*, p.156.

[17] Thoreau managed to do this and he notes the times when work of any kind, whether of the head or hands was given over to the 'bloom of the present moment', Thoreau, *Walden,* p. 156.

[18] John Austin Baker, *The Foolishness of God* (Darton, Longman and Todd, 1970), pp. 385–386.

[19] Theo Hobson has written an interesting and provocative article on this theme. See 'Is it Really so Shameful to Suffer from Liberal Guilt', *The Guardian*, 30 August 2010.

[20] St Augustine, Luther and Calvin are names to be reckoned with here. It has to be said that, in their desire or determination to uphold the sovereignty of God's grace, something vital was forfeited in relation to the more theologically nuanced understanding of humankind, advanced for e.g. in Genesis 1:26 where we are made in God's image and likeness.

[21] St Bonaventura (c.1217–1274) Franciscan theologian and spiritual writer cited in M.A. Screech, *Rabelais and the Challenge of the Gospel,* (Koerner, Baden-Baden and Boux Willer, 1992), p. 64.

[22] Fritz A. Rothschild (ed.), *Between God and Man: An Interpretation of Judaism, from the writings of Abraham J. Heschel* (The Free Press, 1965), p. 236.

[23] Nahman of Bratslav, cited in Sefer Sihot Maharan, 239.

[24] Mark L. Winer, 'Tikkun Olam: A Jewish Theology of 'Repairing the World' in *Theology,* Vol. CX1. No. 864 November/December 2008, p. 439.

[25] The Kabbalah, the Jewish mystical tradition, describes the pristine world as an urn shattered by human enmity and animosity, character-ised by the story of Cain and Abel in Genesis 4:1–16. Interestingly, from a Christian perspective, it is in this passage that 'sin' is mentioned for the first time in the Bible: 'The Lord said to Cain, "Why are you angry, and why has your countenance fallen? If you do well, will you not be accepted? And if you do not do well, sin is lurking at the door; its desire is for you, but you must master it." ' (Gen. 4:6–7).

[26] Winer, 'Tikkun Olam', p. 434.

[27] A recurring theme of this chapter, hence its title, has been inspired by John Berger's latest reflections on our contemporary world. See his *Hold Everything Dear: Dispatches on Survival and Resistance* (Verso, 2007).

[28] It is not only in Genesis or Revelation that we see this truth affirmed. In 1 Kings 4:29–34 we read of the great wisdom of Solomon who spoke 'of trees, from the cedar that is in the Lebanon to the hyssop that grows in the wall'. In the early Christian centuries, theologians of the stature of Origen, Clement of Alexandria and Basil of Neo-Caesarea empha-sised the lessons to be drawn from 'the works of the Lord' and the

wholeness of a creation. Basil wanted his readers to see that every tiny
plant was a reminder of its maker and that 'a single blade of grass is
enough to occupy your whole mind as you contemplate the skill that
produced it'. See Charles Raven, *Natural Religion and Christian Theology*
(Cambridge University Press, 1953), pp. 46–47. Quite by chance, I've
just read that the winning entry in this year's astronomy photographer
of the year competition shows an ancient bristlecone pine against the
Milky Way as a meteor streaks across the sky. A quite breathtaking
photograph. See *The Guardian*, 10 September 2010, pp. 22–23.

[29] Linguistically, *shalom* derives from *shalem*, meaning 'whole' or 'complete'. According to the Kabbalah, the whole world was created
together as a unified whole.

CHAPTER 9

Happy Days: the Persistence of Hope

This final chapter begins with an intriguing tale of three grave stones. The first two can be seen in a painting by Henry Alexander Bowler, entitled *The Doubt: Can These Dry Bones Live?*, painted between 1855 and 1856. The canvas shows a young woman leaning on the tombstone of one John Faithful; inscribed on it is the text: 'I am the resurrection and the life' (John 11:25) — venerable words which carry the religious conviction that ultimately death shall have no dominion. Inscribed on the adjacent stone is the solitary and defiant word 'RESURGAM' ('I shall arise'). This word was frequently inscribed on tombs of the period, and, in the painting, a horse chestnut protrudes from the tomb, and a butterfly, representing the soul, perches on a visible skull. John Faithful, it seems, has placed his hope in Christ. His neighbour, by contrast, appears to have a more attenuated self-belief that without invoking religion, his life will go on beyond the grave. It's a fascinating painting, at one level entirely consonant with traditional Christian teaching and at another pointing futuristically to the fuzzy and disparate beliefs concerning life after death that characterise our own time. In place of 'RESURGAM', we now have a hugely popular poem that is frequently read at funerals and has even been set to music:

> Do not stand at my grave and weep;
> I am not there. I do not sleep.
> I am a thousand winds that blow,
> I am the diamond glints on snow,
> I am the sunlight on ripened grain,
> I am the gentle autumn rain …
> Do not stand at my grave and cry,
> I am not there. I did not die.[1]

We are some distance from Christian orthodoxy here, yet the appeal of the poem to the sorrowing human heart is undeniable, notwithstanding the credibility or otherwise of its evocation of a continuing life that at death is woven into the wider cycle of nature.[2] Its importance and utility lie in another incontrovertible fact that we shall return to later. There is the business, meanwhile, of a third gravestone that can be found in the Cimetière du Montparnasse, Paris. It is a huge slab of polished black granite that bears the name of Samuel Beckett and his time on earth, 1906–1989. There is no verse from scripture or poetry to provide emotional uplift, or any evidence of a personal creed. Instead, at the foot of the grave stands one lone tree.

Beckett is best known for his pessimism and the ways in which he dissects and lays bare the emptiness and fears that attend human wantings and waitings. He was born on Good Friday near Dublin, the son of a quantity surveyor and nurse. In adolescence, he was a pupil at the same school which Oscar Wilde had attended. Unhappy and restless, eight years later he moved to Paris and wrote a study of Proust before travelling through Europe writing poems and stories and doing casual work to survive. The journey furnished him with ideas and characters that eventually found their way into his books and plays. Late in 1937 he returned to Paris, where, in the season of peace and goodwill, he was stabbed and nearly killed by a man who approached him in the street for money. After recovering, Beckett visited his assailant in prison and asked the prisoner why he had attacked him. The man replied 'Je ne sais pas, Monsieur'. During World War II, Beckett joined the French Resistance and was awarded the Croix de Guerre and the Medaille de la Resistance for his efforts in fighting the German occupation. After the war, his plays and novels brought him international fame and, in 1969, he was awarded the Nobel Prize for Literature. It is understood that he gave the prize money away to struggling writers.

Many of Beckett's characters exist and survive in a strange world of bewilderment and sadness, where the tragic and the comic raise the meaning of existence. Quite recently I went to see *Waiting for Godot* in Manchester: a very spare stage, a stranger (Godot) who never comes, two tramps at the end of their tether forever arguing or complaining, and a solitary tree. Time passes and passes, and, outside the frenzy and futility of the conversation, nothing happens. But the talking and the questions go on. The most famous production of *Waiting For Godot* took place in 1957, when a company of actors from the San Francisco Actors' Workshop performed the play before an audience of fourteen hundred convicts at the San Quentin prison. It was a great success. The prisoners understood as well as the tramps, Vladimir and Estragon, that life sometimes entails waiting, killing time and clinging, however tenuously, to the belief that respite may be just around the corner. If not today, then maybe tomorrow.

I have seen other plays by Beckett but, for me, the most unforgettable was the performance of *Happy Days*, featuring Billie Whitelaw in the lead role of Winnie, at the Royal Court Theatre in London in 1979. Beckett directed, and Whitelaw held the audience with her emotional intensity and resolution. Winnie is middle-aged and immobile – buried to her waist in a mound of earth in the first act, buried to her neck in the second. There is only one other character, her husband Willie, and he is largely unseen and silent for most of the play. Like *Godot* there is little by way of excitement or action. Winnie's opening words – 'Another heavenly day' – set the tone for a monologue as she occupies herself with the contents of her enormous handbag. She checks the items – toothbrush, toothpaste, spectacles, a compact mirror, a handkerchief, a music box, a revolver. She opens an umbrella, she prays, reminisces about the past and tries to recall memorable lines that she has once read. Her situation, at once ludicrous and impossible (and therefore true to life as we sometimes actually experience it), does not deter her. She chatters cheerfully on and even dispenses advice to herself: 'How often have I said, in evil hours, sing now Winnie, sing your song, there is nothing else for it.' She does not complain, and, despite her occasional remonstrations with a husband largely tucked away behind a newspaper, by the end of the play Willie honours the bond that binds them together. Dressed to impress in top hat, morning coat and striped trousers, he tries to reach Winnie but then tumbles down the mound enveloping her. She is visibly transformed by his effort and, as she smiles, she urges him on again as she sings the love duet from *The Merry Widow*. The knowledge of his presence is a source of comfort and inspiration to her and the prerequisite for all her 'happy days'. Even though she has little to feel happy about, no day passes without Winnie trying to look her best and carry on.[3]

Beckett does not mock her with the monologue he places on her lips and he is not deriding us for seeing something noble and majestic in her stance. He is, we should recall, a child of Good Friday, sensitive to the often unheeded cry of the maimed, the inarticulate and the decrepit, yet refusing to despair in the face of the void or the prospect of extinction. Paradox surrounds him, and this constitutes part of his fascination and importance for religion. Apparently convinced that much of life is meaningless, he persists in writing a body of poignant and honest work that suggests the opposite, and risks his life to resist the evils of fascism. Never quite free of the insistent question of God or the possibility of 'some great love beyond ourselves that haunts the universe'[4], he seems to say that reality is to be found, endured and overcome in the face of God's apparent absence rather than his presence. A prophet of silence, he is buried in a grave containing little by way of information except his name and length of days. But there is something else recorded there – the name and age of Suzanne Desceveaux-Dumesnil, his lifelong companion who eventually became his wife at a secret civil ceremony in England in 1961. And attending the grave is a single tree, a green testament to the conviction that we must commit ourselves to something important in a chaotic and unjust world where the flame of the human spirit can serve as a shield and sun in the face of adversity and darkness. A single tree symbolising, perhaps, the persistence of hope or the survival of love even in the dust of death.

Beckett is not for the religiously faint-hearted, or believers driven by the lust for certainty in uncertain times. And he does have his blind spots. For all the clues he offers us concerning our deepest predicaments and the preciseness of his humane intelligence, there are things he misses on his journeys. I'm thinking here, for example, of his trek across Europe as a young man that fed the pessimism and the imagination that defined his later writings. It seems clear that along the way he encountered lost souls and experienced what Dr Samuel Johnson once described as 'life's long vacancies', the slow grind of existence that dismays the spirit. Perhaps he was unfortunate in the sameness of his encounters, or maybe he was drawn temperamentally to those at the margins and failed to notice other lives. I'm curious, and I'm speculating because I have just finished a book by another writer who also felt he 'was born lost', but on his travels experienced much that was magical.

John Steinbeck was born in California in 1902, four years before Beckett and, like him, had a thirst for new places, the 'wanderlust' that yearned to be somewhere else. Like Beckett he also longed to see Paris, but he didn't have the price of a ticket. Much later in life, more financially secure and accompanied by his French poodle, Charley, he drives across America from coast to coast, through woods and forests, large cities and spectacular wildernesses. There are moments that belong in *Godot*. Here is Steinbeck desperate for rest and refreshment after driving too long, and coming across the place he needs – a little guest house in New Hampshire with a sign bearing the welcome words 'Open' and 'Vacancy'. He writes in his journal:

> I opened the door and went in. Not a soul was there … I banged on the little bell on the desk, then called out 'Anybody here?' No answer, nothing. I sat down on a stool to await the return of the management. The numbered keys to the little white houses hung on a board. The daylight slipped away and the place darkened. I went outside to collect Charley and to verify my impression that the sign said 'Open' and 'Vacancy'. By now it was getting dark. I brought out a flashlight and looked through the office for a note saying 'Back in ten minutes', but there was none. I felt strangely like a Peeping Tom; I didn't belong there. Then I went outside, fed Charley, made some coffee, and waited.

> It would have been simple to take a key, leave a note on the desk saying that I had done so, and open one of the little houses. It wasn't right. I couldn't do it. On the highway a few cars went by and crossed the bridge over the river, but none turned in. The windows of the office and grill flashed under approaching headlights and then blacked out again. I had planned to eat a light supper and then to fall dog-weary into bed. I made my bed, found I wasn't hungry after all, and lay down. But sleep would not come to me. I listened for the return of the management. At last I lighted my gas mantle and

tried to read, but with listening I could not follow the words.
At last I dozed, awakened in the dark, looked out – nothing,
nobody. My little sleep was troubled and uneasy.

At dawn I arose and created a long, slow, time-wasting breakfast. The sun came up, searching out the windows. I walked
down to the river to keep Charley company, returned, even
shaved and took a sponge bath in a bucket. The sun was well up
by now. I went to the office and entered. The refrigerator
hummed, the faucet dripped into the cold soapy water of the
sink. A new-born, heavy-winged fat fly crawled fretfully over a
plastic pie cover. At nine-thirty I drove away and no one had
come, nothing had moved. The sign still read 'Open' and
'Vacancy'. I drove across the iron bridge, rattling the steel-
tread plates. The empty place disturbed me deeply, and, come
to think of it, still does.[5]

I'm fascinated by this vignette with its intimations of hospitality, its
silence and, finally, in the face of all the tantalising questions it raises
and an apparent absence where there should by all accounts be a
presence, I'm intrigued that the sign still cries 'Welcome'. Steinbeck
shares other disarming moments with us and we are told much
concerning the hopes and dreams and quiet desperation that populate the changing landscape. There are great silences too – sometimes in the forests or in the coffee houses and roadside diners where
early morning waitresses lead lonely lives. And there is silence of
another kind that, as far as my reading of Beckett has taken me, is not
to be found in his work. After a night of desolate loneliness, Steinbeck meets a clan of itinerant Canuck migrant labourers harvesting
potatoes. He is made welcome, so much so that after supper he
opens a bottle of old and expensive brandy normally reserved for
'weddings, frost bite and heart attacks'. The cognac is passed first to
the patriarch in the group with surprising and endearing results:

The old man smiled so sweetly that for the first time I could see
he lacked front teeth. The brother-in-law growled in his throat
like a happy tomcat and the pregnant ladies twittered like
alouettes singing to the sun. I handed John a corkscrew while I
laid out the crystal – three plastic coffee cups, a jelly glass, a

shaving mug, and several wide-mouthed pill bottles. I emptied
their capsules into a saucepan and rinsed out the odor of wheat
germ with water from the tap. The cognac was very, very good,
and from the first muttered '*Santé*' and the first clicking sip you
could feel the Brotherhood of Man growing ... They refused
seconds and I insisted. And the division of thirds was put on the
basis that there wasn't enough to save. And with a few divided
drops of that third there came a triumphant human magic that
can bless a house, or a truck for that matter – nine people
gathered in complete silence and the nine parts making a whole
as surely as my arms and legs are part of me, separate and
inseparable.[6]

It seems that the world can sometimes be a wedding where convivi-
ality and human community combine to become a form of benediction. Beckett is largely a stranger to such a world but his own point of
entry is no less valuable. In the bleakness of his landscape, where
often it is only pained conversation that keeps people together, hope
is not abandoned and the possibility of decency endures. It is a tree,
not a flower which fades, that is planted at his grave – a living thing
dedicated to the future in the cathedral hush of a cemetery.

Beckett is good for us because in a wholly unique way he records
faithfully what he sees – the endless agitations that shape our lives.
He does not want us to be deceived concerning such things, for it is
only in the recognition and acceptance of their existence that the
heart of the human condition can be understood. But alongside these
brute facts there persists in his work a rumour, a barely believable
but tenaciously held hope that somehow we rise and go on. He
understands the meaning of that blazing word 'RESURGAM' which
opened this chapter, and, if he is agnostic concerning 'the resurrection and the life' inscribed on the adjacent gravestone of that Victo-
rian cemetery, he recognises the legitimacy of the human heart in its
insistence that things should go well and that conscience shies away
from anything which denies this possibility. Even the overtly senti-
mental poem 'Do not Stand at my Grave and Weep' would not, I
think, be dismissed out of hand by him. In its claim to a particular
form of immortality, he would see this as an expression of human
longing – that hope or hunger which by its very persistence presup-
poses the existence of bread.

We are on religious ground here, and, in consequence, Beckett and Christianity are not as far apart as is sometimes supposed. It seems to me a needless over-simplification to classify him as a playwright concerned only with the absurd and tragic features of life. He is engaged in the most fundamental of human endeavours, not far behind the quests for shelter, food and community – the search for truth concerning the visible and invisible world. Rather like the Christian faith throughout its history, his work is 'a perpetual argument about meaning and reality'[7]. As a child of Good Friday, he knows that Jesus is brought before Pontius Pilate to be tried. In the midst of one of the most significant human exchanges ever recorded, Jesus replies to Pilate that 'I came into the world to testify to the truth' (John 18:37). In a tone that is hard to interpret – sincere, cynical, world-weary? – Pilate replies: 'What is truth?' (John 18:38). Jesus does not reply and the question is left unresolved, to wait upon the verdict of all seekers who come after. The Gospel of John is enigmatic: it uses terms drawn from common experience – bread, water, light, life, shepherd, door, way – to make the significance of Jesus clear. But it is also a profoundly mystical text: it grapples with the mystery of the 'Word made flesh' and the haunting possibilities of a dark and impenetrable drama where, crazily and tragically, the beloved Son of God becomes the object of persecution and unbelief (John Chapters 5 to 12). This is a narrative suited to Beckett's pen – a world gone wrong, a central character marked by grief and sorrow, an unanswered question that touches upon the misery and injustice of life and how we are to respond to such things. Here words of scripture can form part of the playwright's hinterland[8], for they deal with the actuality of our lives: the deep ache we experience, the quiver of sharp and enduring questions, our immortal longings and the desire that they should be satisfied and our hope that ultimately we are neither disappointed nor confounded.

If Beckett cannot accept that in some sense Christ's suffering and death make us free and open up new vistas of life (John 20:31), he is not disposed to abandon the question of truth and does not embrace a disaffected or nihilistic world view where hope is nothing more than a longing for things that will never happen. There are no happy endings in Beckett but there are happy days when, even in our lostness or rage, there is a challenge to begin again, to rise up, to wait with expectancy for something transcendent that will redeem our human exile. To wait, in other words, in hope for some saving work even when our minds are in hell or close to desolation. In pointing us to the persistence of hope that is such a marked feature of our humanity, Beckett comes to us as a strange and unexpected ally or fellow traveller. With St Paul and the prophets and the psalmists of old, with all those who have walked and watched in the dark, with ourselves and our wounding contradictions, he is a 'prisoner of hope'[9].

In the book of Isaiah, in exile and far from home, the Israelite prisoners come to the prophet and ask: 'Watchman, what of the night?' – how long must we endure it? The watchman answers: 'The morning is coming but it is still night. If you will enquire, come back again' (Isa. 21:12). There is no prophetic answer to the question of how long their time of distress will last. There is instead the require-ment to come back again, to persist in a 'hope against hope', a hope where there is nothing else to hope for. It is an intensely human experience well documented by Beckett and our religious texts. The great Reformation theologian, John Calvin, captures the tension well:

> To us is promised eternal life – but to us, the dead. We are preached a blessed resurrection – but in the meantime we are surrounded by corruption. We are called just – and yet what dwells in us is sin. We hear of inexpressible blessedness – but in the meantime we are bowed down under unending misery. We are promised a superfluity of all good things – yet we are rich only in hunger and thirst. What would become of us if we did not obstinately cling to hope, and if our minds did not hasten along the paths lit up for us by God's Word and Spirit right through the darkness, beyond this world?[10]

Human beings are the awkward and resilient ones who refuse to relinquish the torch. Hope is the last thing to die, even when the flame burns low or some lose heart and give up. As long as we breathe, we hope, and its absence makes life unendurable. All of us can still remember the human drama of the 33 Chilean miners trapped in the bowels of the earth in the summer of 2010. Everyone eventually got out alive, and their deliverance was spoken of in miraculous terms. But a less reported fact moved me no less: when everything still seemed very uncertain concerning their safety, one of the younger miners was informed that his wife had given birth to their child. She had been given a provisional name but he sent a message to the surface from the darkest of places. She was to be called Hope.

Steinbeck would like this story, and he has one of his own to complement it. As he comes to the end of his long journey in search of America, he enters the South and sees first hand the blight of prejudice and segregation. After a particularly unpleasant experience concerning a man who has accused him of being a 'Nigger lover', he picks up one more passenger between Jackson and Montgomery – a young Negro student, more than ready to discuss the burden of racism, the teaching of Martin Luther King and his own desire for action and justice:

> We talked of many things then. He was a passionate and articulate young man with anxiety and fierceness just below the surface. But when I dropped him in Montgomery he leaned through the window of the cab and he laughed. 'I'm ashamed', he said. 'It's just selfishness. But I want to see it – me – not dead. Here! Me! I want to see it – soon' And then he swung around and wiped his eyes with his hand and he walked quickly away.[11]

With his impatience, his thirst for conversation and his longing to see salvation, we see a young man locked into an oppressive present but living in the hope and promise of a future that stands in contradiction to the reality of his present experience. In concrete terms, he has little to support his conviction. Not far away, a crowd of white people has been screaming and shouting outside a local school as 'the littlest Negro girl you ever saw, dressed in shining starchy white ... with new shoes on her feet'[12] tries to make her way into class escorted by a phalanx of guards. But this older and fiercer student has three fountain pens in his breast pocket, he is carrying a sheaf of papers, his eyes are fixed on a better day and he has received kindness from a stranger. There will be a tomorrow that will not suffer the same mistakes and an end, so he believes, to the twisted, bitter lies told by one race about another. He will rise.

Along with faith and love, hope abides, and its persistence proves more contagious than despair. Human beings, believers or other-wise, are 'prisoners of hope', sometimes barely sustained by nothing more than hints and guesses, but unwilling to accept the conclusion that life is absurd and their only sure prospect is extinction. Such a conclusion is unmerited and leaves too much unexplained. It fails to reflect our deepest, truest and best intuitions that our earth-bound longings are more than wishful thinking and that hope, however audacious, will not finally prove illusory.

As to the source of such intuitions and longings, the 'still small voice' of religion, schooled in realism for so many long centuries by prayer, discipline, failure, disappointment and silence, rests its case on the two hands of God – on Christ, the 'true light which enlightens everyone' (John 1:9), and the anointing Spirit which renews 'the dullness of our blinded sight'. The record of God's pilgrim people begins with Abraham, who 'hoping against hope believed that he would become the father of many nations' (Rom. 4:18). It continues with the children of Israel, brought out of bondage and provided with sustenance in their wilderness years before being brought to an 'exceedingly good land'. But, as we read earlier, this is not a senti-mental story. They will suffer exile in the city of Babylon and will weep by its waters as they remember the gates of Zion (Ps. 137:1).Yet with all means of support swept away – the monarchy, the temple, the feasts and fasts and ritual sacrifices – they will wait in hope:

> The thought of my affliction and my
> homelessness is wormwood and gall
> My soul continually thinks of it and
> is bowed down within me. But this
> I call to mind and therefore I have hope.
> The steadfast love of the Lord never ceases,
> his mercies never come to an end;
> they are new every morning;
> great is your faithfulness.
> 'The Lord is my portion' says my soul,
> 'therefore I will hope in him'.

(Lam. 3:19–24)

They are upheld by that which sustains spiritual luminaries such as Isaiah, Jeremiah, Job, Paul … indeed, the whole 'cloud of witnesses' recorded by the writer of Hebrews (Chapter 11). Their faces are set to the shape of God's future: by faith they commit themselves to things beyond the present horizon – to 'the glory that is to be revealed' (Rom. 8:18) that is sensed by 'hope alone'. They trust that they are heirs to a divine promise and that another world is possible in the here and now, 'a new heaven and a new earth' (Rev. 21:1) when the whole creation will be renewed and transformed by God (Rom. 8:18–21). They believe in a fuller life, a life before death, because their hearts are fixed on One who has invited them to new, unfettered horizons, where the 'iron laws' of injustice no longer prevail.[13] The God of Israel's exodus is now found by Christians to be the God of Christ's resurrection, and is known in the wind and flame of the Holy Spirit that blows and burns where it chooses and fills all those who believe with hope (Rom. 15:13).

The Spirit blows freely and makes itself known as the ambassador of the God of hope. In Paris, Beckett would sometimes sit with other renowned writers, occasionally conversing but often silent and unhappy. In the same city, the great artist Marc Chagall moved amongst tradesmen, waiters, market workers and peasants, and found hovering around them an astonishing 'freedom light' which he had never seen elsewhere: 'this light passed easily onto the canvases of the great French masters and was *reborn in art*'[14].

For believers, this is the light which enlightens and enlivens everything and leads us on. Through prayer, attentiveness and sacrifice, it passes through us 'on to God's canvas which is human history' and becomes the 'midwife of a new world'[15], a newly-imagined future in accord with the purposes of God. Here, in this final scene, it is the artist not the playwright who brings us good news. Hope benignly holds us captive but it also saves and redeems (Rom. 8:24).

Notes

[1]   The poem has been attributed to a soldier going to Northern Ireland and Mary Elizabeth Frye (1904–2004), and features on Howard Goodall's *Eternal Light: A Requiem* (EMI Classics, 2008).

[2]   Tom Wright takes up this issue from a Christian perspective in his *Surprised by Hope* (SPCK, 2007), pp. 13–19.

3   Although scholars believed for years that *Happy Days* was futuristically inspired by the 1970s US sitcom of the same name, recent research reveals that Beckett took the play's title from Jack Yellen and Milton Ager's 1929 song, 'Happy Days Are Here Again'.

4   Quote of Bishop Richard Holloway cited in *The Churches' Fellowship For Psychical and Spiritual Studies Quarterly Review,* No. 225, Autumn 2010, p. 35

5   John Steinbeck, *Travels with Charley in Search of America* (Penguin Classics, 2000), pp. 58–59.

6   Steinbeck, *Travels,* p. 54.

7   Quotation of Diarmaid MacCulloch, *Christianity: The First Three Thousand Years,* cited by Jon Meacham in book review 'Thine is the Kingdom', *The New York Times*, 4 April 2010. In this respect the novelist John Wain describes the writer's task as 'a matter of feeling and living at the required depth, fending off the continual temptation to be glib and shallow, to appeal to the easily aroused response, to be evasive and shirk the hard issues. It is a matter of training oneself to live with reality'. From his autobiography *Sprightly Running*, cited by Timothy Gorringe, *Redeeming Time: Atonement through Education* (Darton, Longman and Todd, 1986), p. 133.

8   As a geographical term, hinterland is the land or district behind the borders of a coastal river. In a further sense, it has come to mean an individual's breadth and depth of knowledge of matters outside their immediate experience or expertise.

9   See Ephesians 3:1, 4:1, Philemon 1:1. Paul frequently refers to himself as a prisoner of Christ or a prisoner in the Lord. In either case he is a 'prisoner of hope' and 'hope does not disappoint us' (Rom. 5:5).

10 J. Calvin, *In Omnes Novi Testamenti Epistolas Commentarii,* vol. 11, Halle, 1834, 484.

11 Steinbeck, *Travels,* p. 206.

12 Steinbeck, *Travels,* p. 194

13 See Jurgen Moltmann, *In the End – the Beginning* (SCM Press, 2004), pp. 87–95.

14 M. Chagall, in Sorlier (ed.), *Chagall* (London, 1979), p. 8.

15 Gorringe, *Redeeming Time,* p. 134.

Select Bibliography

Augustine, *City of God,* Book 15.
——*Confessions,* Book X, Penguin Classics, 1961.

Baker, J. A., *The Foolishness of God,* Darton, Longman and Todd, 1970.
Barr, J., *Holy Scripture: Canon, Authority, Criticism,* Oxford, 1983.
Berger, J., *Hold Everything Dear: Dispatches on Survival and Resistance,* Verso, 2007.
Berger, P. L., *Redeeming Laughter: The Comic Dimension of Human Experience,* Walter de Gruyter, 1997.
Berlin, I., *The Crooked Timber of Humanity: Chapters in the History of Ideas,* Vintage Books, 1992.
Blake, W., *The Marriage of Heaven and Hell,* c.1790.
Blocher, H., *Original Sin: Illuminating the Riddle,* Apollos, 1997.
Bramble, F., *The Strange Case of Deacon Brodie,* Hamish Hamilton.
Bridges, R., *I Love All Beauteous Things,* 1876.
Brown, P., *The Body and Society,* Faber & Faber, 1989.
Bunyan, J., *The Pilgrim's Progress,* first published in 1678.
Butler, M., *Romantics, Rebels and Reactionaries: English Literature and its Background 1760–1830,* Oxford University Press, 1981.
Byatt, A. S., and Wood, H. H. (eds.), *Memory An Anthology,* Chatto & Windus, 2008.

Caritas in Veritate: Charity in Truth, Veritas Publications, 2009.
Carver, R., *A New Path to the Waterfall: Last Poems,* Collins Harvill, 1990.

Dales, D., *Glory Descending: Michael Ramsey and his Writings,* Canterbury Press, 2005.
Davies, J. G., *Pilgrimage Yesterday and Today: Why? Where? How?,* SCM Press Ltd, 1988.
de Botton, A., *How Proust can Change Your Life,* Picador, 1997.
Dillistone, F. W., *The Christian Understanding of Atonement,* Nisbet, 1968.

Dix, G., *The Shape of the Liturgy,* A & C Black, 1945.
Donoghue, D., *Speaking of Beauty,* Yale University Press, 2003.

Eco, U. (ed.), *On Beauty: A History of a Western Idea,* Secker & Warburg, 2004.

Farrar, F. W., *Eternal Hope,* London, 1892.
Frayn, M., *The Human Touch: Our Part in the Creation of a Universe,* Faber & Faber, 2006.

Garner, R., *The Big Questions: Believing with Heart and Mind,* SPCK, 1995.
Ginsberg, L., *The Legends of the Jews,* Philadelphia, 1913.
Gorringe, T., *Redeeming Time: Atonement through Education,* Darton, Longman and Todd, 1986.

Happold, F. C., *Prayer and Meditation,* Pelican, 1971.
Herbert, G., *The Complete English Works,* Everyman's Library, 1995.
Hymns Ancient and Modern Revised, William Clowes & Sons Ltd, 1922.

Kundera, M., *Testaments Betrayed,* Faber & Faber, 2004.

Layard, R., *Happiness: Lessons from a New Science,* Penguin, 2005.
Leech, K., *We Preach Christ Crucified,* Darton, Longman and Todd, 2006.

MacKinnon, D., *Explorations in Theology,* SCM Press, 1979.
Manguel, A., *A Reader on Reading,* Yale University Press, 2010.
Margalit, A., *The Ethics of Memory,* Harvard Press, 2003.
Moltmann, J., *In the End – the Beginning,* SCM Press, 2004.
Motion, A., *The Cinder Path,* Faber & Faber, 2009.

O'Connell, R. J., *Art and the Christian Intelligence in St Augustine,* Blackwell, 1978.

Petrement, S., *Simone Weil,* Mowbrays, 1976
Polkinghorne, J. (ed.), *The Work of Love: Creation as Kenosis,* Eerdmans Publishing/SPCK, 2001.
Pope, A., *An Essay on Man,* Epistle 2.

Raven, C., *Natural Religion and Christian Theology,* Cambridge University Press, 1953.
Ricks, C. (ed.), *The Oxford Book of English Verse,* Oxford, 1999.

Rinpoche, S., *The Tibetan Book of Living and Dying,* Rider & Co, 1998.

Rothschild, F.A. (ed.), *Between God and Man:An Interpretation of Judaism, from the Writings of Abraham J. Heschel,* The Free Press 1965.

Rubin, M., *Mother of God:A History of theVirgin Mary,* Allen Lane, 2009.

Sartre, J. P., *Cahiers Pour une Morale,* Paris, 1983.

Schoch, R. S., *The Secrets of Happiness:Three ThousandYears of Searching for the Good Life,* Profile, 2006.

Screech, M.A., *Laughter at the Foot of the Cross,* Penguin Books, 1997.

——*Rabelais and the Challenge of the Gospel,* Koerner, Baden-Baden and Boux Willer, 1992.

Shank, D., *The Forgetting,* Flamingo Press, 2003.

Sibley, E., *The Cello Suites: In Search of a Baroque Masterpiece,* Harvill Secker, 2010.

Soelle, D., *The Silent Cry,* Augsburg Fortress, 2001.

Stangroom J. & Garvey J. (eds.), *The Great Philosophers,* Eagle Editions Ltd, 2006.

Steinbeck, J., *Travels with Charley in Search of America,* Penguin Classics, 2000.

Stevenson, R. L., *Dr Jekyll and Mr Hyde,* Dorling Kindersley, 1997.

Thoreau, H. D., *Walden,* Fall River Press, 2008 edition.

——*Walden and Civil Disobedience,* Penguin Classics, 1986.

Vanstone, W. H., *Love's Endeavour, Love's Expense:The Response of Being to the Love of God,* Darton, Longman and Todd, 1977.

Vernon, M., *42:DeepThought on Life, the Universe and Everything,* OneWorld, 2008.

Ware, K., *The Orthodox Way,* Mowbray, 1979.

Weil, S., *Waiting on God:The Essence of HerThought,* Collins Fontana, 1973.

Wengert, T. J. (ed.), *The Pastoral Luther: Essays on Martin Luther's Practical Theology,* Eerdmans, 2009.

Williams, R., *Open to Judgement: Sermons and Addresses,* Darton, Longman and Todd, 1994.

Winkett, L., *Our Sound is Our Wound:Contemplative Listening in a Noisy World,* Continuum, 2010.

Winterson, J., *Art Objects: Essays on Ecstasy and Effrontery,* Jonathan Cape, 1995.

——*Oranges are Not the Only Fruit,* Vintage, 2001.

Woolf, V., *Moments of Being,* Hogarth Press, 1985 edition.
Wright, T., *Surprised By Hope,* SPCK, 2007.

Yeats, W. B., *The Collected Poems of W. B. Yeats*, London, 1933.